D1351507

THE
GOLDEN
MONARCH

MICHAEL CARTER

THE GOLDEN MONARCH

Tutankhamun
The Man Behind the Mask

THE DOLPHIN PRESS
CHRISTCHURCH

First published in Great Britain by
The Dolphin Press, Dolphin House, Beaulieu Avenue
Christchurch, Hants.

ISBN 0 85642 003 4

First impression April, 1972
Second impression May, 1972

Printed in Great Britain
by The Rochdale Times Ltd.
Rochdale, Lancs.

Bound by James Burn at
Esher, Surrey

CONTENTS

CHAPTER ONE

★

DISCOVERY

"At first I could see nothing, the hot air escaping from the chamber causing the candle flame to flicker, but presently, as my eyes grew accustomed to the light, details of the room within emerged slowly from the mist, strange animals, statues and gold — everywhere the glint of gold."* With these words Howard Carter describes his first glimpse of what is undoubtedly the greatest archaeological discovery ever made, not only to Egyptology, but to the world of archaeology in general. Nothing before nor since, has ever equalled and probably never will equal the splendour and magnificence of the tomb of Tutankhamun, a little known Pharaoh of the 18th Dynasty. Until then, he was known only by one or two minor objects that had lain in museums attracting little attention, but from November 1922 his name was a household word. He was Egyptology.

Our story, however, does not start here. It starts in the British Museum, where young Howard Carter was employed as a draughtsman to ink in tracings of tomb sketches made by the Egyptologist, Percy Newberry. He so excelled that in 1892 he went to Egypt as Newberry's assistant, where he was to have his first taste of practical archaeology by digging under the great Egyptologist Sir William Flinders Petrie.

Since his first visit to Egypt, Carter had longed to dig in The Valley of the Kings, the Biban-el-Moluk, at Thebes, a royal necropolis hewn out of the barren sides of a desiccated valley 600 miles up the River Nile in Upper Egypt, near the small town of Luxor. An inconspicuous cemetery, it was the final resting place of some of the best known Pharaohs of the New Kingdom, (1567-1085 B.C.) who, for the security of their immortal remains, sought to hide them in rock-cut tombs in The Valley, rather than to advertise them with great pyramids of stone. In 1907 he began to excavate in association with George Herbert, fifth Earl of Carnarvon, a wealthy patron of Egyptology, in the hope that they might eventually be granted a concession there. It was an ambition held by Carter since the time he was Inspector of the Antiquities Department, when he had found and superintended the clearing of two tombs in The Valley for an American dilettante, Mr. Theodore Davis.

For several relatively uneventful years from 1907-1914, Carter and Lord Carnarvon had to content themselves with excavating other parts of the Theban necropolis, until in 1914, the discovery of the tomb of Amenophis I at the Drah Abu'l Negga foothills, aroused their thoughts of excavating in The Valley. By this time, Theodore Davis, who still held the concession, had published his conclusions that The Valley was exhausted, and although somewhat loath to give up the site, the concession was signed in favour of Carter and Carnarvon in June 1914. Despite the general opinion that The Valley had yielded up all its secrets, a view that had been held for some years, Carter was convinced that there were still areas that had never been properly examined, since they were covered with the debris of previous excavations. He was convinced for a number of reasons. Theodore Davis, towards the end of his campaign in The Valley, had found hidden under a rock, a faience cup bearing the name of Tutankhamun. Not far away, he had also come upon a small pit-tomb containing an unnamed alabaster figure and a broken wooden box in which were fragments of gold foil, bearing the name of Tutankhamun and his Queen, Ankhesenamun. On the basis of this he claimed to have found the tomb of Tutankhamun! Also, in his earlier years of excavation, Davis had found a cache of large pottery jars, with inscriptions on their shoulders, which seemed to contain nothing but broken pottery and fragments of linen. Little attention was paid to them until Davis gave permission for them to be taken to the Metropolitan Museum of Art, New York, for a thorough examination of their contents. This examination proved extraordinarily rewarding, revealing not only seals and a linen head shawl bearing the latest known date of the reign of Tutankhamun, but floral collars of a kind worn by mourners. To Carter, this much underrated find represented the funerary material of Tutankhamun, that once used had been stored away in jars, and perhaps a clue to the location of his tomb.

How right he was.

Another piece of evidence that was to further associate Tutankhamun with that particular part of The Valley, was the discovery by Davis of the funerary remains in Tomb 55. The contents seemed to have been hurriedly brought to a place of safety from Akhetaten, (present day Tell-el-Amarna) the capital of the heretic king Akhenaten. This tomb plays an important part in our story and we shall return to it later. Carter was reasonably sure that Tutankhamun had been responsible for this, as a number of clay seals bearing his cartouche had been found in the debris of the tomb.

Now that the concession was theirs the path before

them seemed clear, although extremely arduous, for many thousands of tons of debris had to be removed before they could even hope to find anything. But for Carter and Carnarvon their supreme gift of patience was to be their greatest ally, not only during their search, but during the many trials and tribulations they would have to endure on the discovery of the tomb. It was certainly needed now, for with the outbreak of war in 1914 hopes of a concentrated campaign had to be postponed. Although Carter managed to snatch short periods to continue his work, the real campaign in The Valley did not open until June 1917.

Faced with the task of investigating beneath the rubble of previous excavators, Carter and Carnarvon decided from the beginning that the only satisfactory thing to do, was to dig systematically down to bedrock over a chosen area. This area was to be a triangle of ground defined simply by the already discovered tombs of Ramesses II, Merenptah, and Ramesses VI. And so they began. Carter's methods, inspired by the work of Sir Flinders Petrie, were painstakingly meticulous. He made a large scale plan of the whole area which he divided into sections, and after investigating an area would tick off the corresponding section, in this way ensuring that he did not miss one square inch of The Valley floor. It was a season's work to clear most of the upper layers in this area and continue the excavation up to the foot of the tomb of Ramesses VI. Here they came across a series of workmen's huts, built over masses of flint boulders, which Carter noted usually indicated in The Valley the proximity of a tomb.

By the end of the 1919-20 season this triangular area had been completely exhausted, and to the dismay of Carter and Carnarvon no tomb had been found. In fact the most exciting of their finds had been a cache of alabaster jars bearing the names of Ramesses II, and Merenptah his son !

They then spent the next two seasons investigating the small lateral valley that held the tomb of Tuthmosis III, the only finds being of academic rather than of intrinsic value. They had by now spent six seasons in The Valley, and after what seemed many wasted years there was great debate as to whether there was any point in going on. Spirits must indeed have been low. For Carter himself, the fact that as long as there was a single area in The Valley untouched, there was a risk worth taking, and, anyway, there were still the workmen's huts at the foot of the tomb of Ramesses VI to be thoroughly investigated. Luckily for Egyptology and the world, Carter's arguments were convincing and it was decided to devote just one more season to the area. But they had problems. If they were to investigate this last area in The Valley, the access to the tomb of Ramesses VI would have to be cut off from the many visitors that flocked there each season, and so, in order to cause the least disruption it was decided to begin the season early.

At the beginning of November 1922, Howard Carter was on the threshold of the world's most spectacular archaeological find, a discovery that was to drastically change his life and bring before his eyes wondrous sights that he could not have visualised even in his wildest dreams. How could he have suspected, or dared hope, that in this final season, in this last desperate attempt to find the tomb for which he had been searching for so long, it would emerge beneath the first workmen's hut they chose to investigate. On the morning of November 4th there it was, a step cut in the rock beneath the first of the huts built over 3,000 years earlier by the workmen of Ramesses VI, during the cutting of his tomb. There, just 13 feet below the

11

entrance to Ramesses' tomb, was the realisation of all Carter had dreamed of in his many years of systematic searching. We can imagine how he felt, as during the daylight of November 4th and most of November 5th the workmen dug feverishly, almost as excited as Carter himself, to reveal what looked more and more like a sunken stairway entrance, typical of tombs in The Valley. During this day and a half, and indeed for many days to come, until he could see the evidence with his own eyes, Howard Carter must have tried to prepare himself for a great disappointment ahead, for disappointment had been the theme of his work in The Valley. The feeling that was haunting him was that when excavated the tomb might prove to be incomplete like that of Tuthmosis III, which he had excavated some years previously. There was also the possibility that even if it was complete it might never have been used, might only contain a few miscellaneous objects, or have been plundered beyond recognition.

Excitedly, yet with the care that after years of systematic work was not to be abandoned, they dug, as step followed step. Soon they found themselves entering the side of a small hillock, which as they excavated became a roofed-in passage 10 feet high by 6 feet wide. Step followed step. By the twelfth step they came across the top of a sealed doorway. After brushing away some of the rubble, Carter eagerly examined the seals on the top of the doorway. He recognised the seal of the royal necropolis, the jackal and nine captives, and realized he had two important pieces of evidence. One, that the tomb was important enough to bear the seal of the royal necropolis and two, that the entrance had been hidden both from previous excavators and tomb robbers, by the workmen's huts constructed for the work on the tomb of Ramesses VI, and could not have been robbed after the 20th Dynasty. Although he did not know until later, this sealed doorway bore the most important clue of all, the seal of Tutankhamun. As he saw that some of the plaster had fallen away near the lintel at the top of the door, Carter could not resist the temptation of making a hole large enough to put his torch through. Beyond this door there was a passage completely filled with rubble, as protection against robbers. Could the tomb be intact?

Then, at a time when the discovery was becoming more and more exciting, Carter did something that he was to do, for various reasons, several times as work progressed, during the years that followed. He filled in the excavation and went home. In a situation when most people, and indeed most excavators of the period, would have torn down that sealed doorway in an uncontrollable desire to reach what lay inside, Howard Carter waited. In this case he waited for Lord Carnarvon, his associate and patron, who was not in Egypt but in England and who must be present at the culmination of six years' work.

On November 6th, with the passage filled in as if it had never been discovered, and the most trustworthy of workmen on guard, Carter cabled Lord Carnarvon in England. He also cabled a colleague, Callender, as he was realizing that he was going to need help. While waiting for the arrival of Carnarvon, he and Callender made various preparations so that as soon as his patron arrived the work could proceed.

By November 24th, Carnarvon with his daughter, Lady Evelyn Herbert, had arrived, the excavation reopened and the work continued, to reveal a full sixteen steps with the sealed doorway beyond. At this point Carter's heart sank, for it was clear that the tomb had been plundered as the door showed signs of being opened and closed. A seal of Tutankhamun seemed to have been original, although the necropolis seal was made at the time of re-closing, perhaps a favourable omen, for it was doubtful if re-sealing would have taken place if the tomb had been completely robbed.

Having recorded and photographed the seals and made good provision for a replacement door, the excavators removed the door and set upon clearing the rubble, potsherds, jar sealings, alabaster vases whole and broken, and painted pottery fragments, that filled the passage from floor to ceiling for a full thirty feet from the outer door. Then before them another door.

Seeing in front of him again, on this the second door, all the signs of the plunderers, Carter was sure that beyond was but a collection of salvaged miscellaneous objects. Here for better or worse was the decisive moment, and they knew it, as with trembling hands Carter made a hole in the door large enough to pass a candle through. There was no rubble behind this door. There were no poisonous gases. What was behind the door was to stagger the world and give Howard Carter and his four anxious colleagues the most remarkable day of their lives. It was November 26th 1922, when Carter, hardly daring to breathe, put a candle through the hole in the door and peered into the darkness. He wrote later :

"At first I could see nothing, the hot air escaping from the chamber causing the candle flame to flicker, but presently, as my eyes grew accustomed to the light, details of the room within emerged slowly from the mist, strange animals, statues, and gold — everywhere the glint of gold."*

By this time Carnarvon could restrain himself no longer,

"Can you see anything?" he inquired. After a pause of what must have seemed minutes Carter replied,

"Yes, wonderful things."

* Howard Carter and A. C. Mace "The Tomb of Tut-Ankh-Amen" Cassell, London, 1923.

CHAPTER TWO

★

TREASURE

The self control exerted by the members of the party, amidst the euphoria that followed is amazing. For Carter himself admits that all his years of archaeological training were for a brief moment pushed aside and replaced with the feelings of a treasure hunter — but only momentarily.

Before them, through the small hole lit by the flickering light of the candle was a kaleidoscope of objects. Here and there the dancing flash of gilt in the darkness. The many shapes of an endless series of objects combined in the dim light to create a bizarre effect. It was impossible to separate individual pieces, everything was wondrous. It was almost like looking into another world. It was another world, separated from our own by over 3,000 years and yet undisturbed during this time, it looked like only yesterday that the last priest had left the tomb.

As they became accustomed to the excitement of the moment, so their eyes became more accustomed to the shapes before them, gradually becoming recognisable as individual objects. The first to catch their attention were three magnificent gilt couches, their sides in the form of weird animals. Then, close by, two human shapes could be seen, figures of the King. They were dark, in fact they were black, with gold kilts and sandals. They stood facing each other, mace and staff in hand, silently guarding the tomb.

Each time they looked they could see something different. Objects of all kinds, some of breathtaking beauty, shrines, a golden inlaid throne, carved chairs, numerous small treasures and at the side of the chamber, a tangled mass of overturned chariots. Even relating the event all these years later, it is impossible to mention everything, for the inventory of the chamber would fill a book.

So great was the effect on the onlookers, that they failed to notice that one very important item was missing, the sarcophagus or coffin. There was no trace of a mummy anywhere. When this fact finally registered, they reviewed the situation in front of them. Slowly in the dim light the answer became clear. Between the two black figures of the King was another sealed doorway. This wonderful treasury was but an antechamber! What lay beyond that door ? With hearts pounding and imaginations running wild, they could not possibly have guessed, for even their wildest dreams were to be surpassed.

With all this before them, for the second time during the excavation Carter sealed the hole, secured the wooden grille that had been fitted in place of the outer doorway, checked the guard, and with the rest of the party rode silently away on his donkey. He had little sleep that night.

The following day, November 27th, after arrangements had been made to connect the tomb to the electric supply of The Valley in order to ensure proper lighting, they continued work. The door was photographed and carefully removed, and for the first time for centuries mortal men once more entered the tomb and breathed the air that was last tasted by the priests of the necropolis all those years ago.

Even now it was difficult to suppress their excitement,

but one disappointment awaited them. They examined the sealed and plastered doorway that they had seen the day before and found to their dismay that tomb robbers had entered the inner chamber. For this door too had been re-sealed. Once again they were not the first. They wondered what lay beyond. Their immediate reaction was to remove the door and settle the matter without further ado, but this was impossible as it would have destroyed a number of objects lying nearby. Moving things too was out of the question, as much scientific information would be lost. It was clear that all the objects in the antechamber would have to be recorded and photographed, and the entire chamber emptied before they could proceed further.

Having realized that their work for the time being lay in the antechamber, they began to make a systematic appraisal of the contents of the room. It was then that the full impact of their discovery dawned upon them. The whole chamber was literally crammed with treasure. Each piece under ordinary circumstances would have sent an Egyptologist's pulse racing, but altogether it was quite overpowering. Carter now knew that this was going to be no quick operation; it would take more than one season at least to clear the antechamber, probably three or four. Many of the objects were in an extremely fragile condition and would need treatment before they could be removed.

The party wandered about the chamber in complete amazement. They were seeing things never even visualised before, seeing aspects of Egyptian art far more advanced than had been thought possible. Carter knew that in more than one way this tomb was going to affect Egyptology, most of what he saw before him would completely revolutionise all the old ideas.

Nearly all the objects, they noticed, bore the name of Tutankhamun, as did the sealed door that they had examined when they entered the tomb. While looking under one of the animal couches one of the party made a further discovery. There was another doorway! Sealed like the others, it too had been broken through but unlike the others, the hole had not been repaired and it was possible to look inside. Ever so gently they edged their way under the couches, until they could insert their portable light through the hole into the other chamber. Conditioned by what they had seen in the antechamber, they expected something of an anti-climax. What they saw, however, surprised even them.

One of the tomb robbers must have broken into the chamber and in a frenzied search to find small easily removed objects of value, had ransacked the place. Everything was topsy-turvy as if it had been struck by a tornado. Boxes had been emptied, and their contents strewn over the floor. Once his eyes were accustomed to the chaos, Carter's attention was caught by a beautiful painted box, as fine as one he had seen in the antechamber. He noticed other things too; a beautiful ivory chair, alabaster and faience vases of exquisite shapes, a gaming board in carved and coloured ivory, leather work, wood, ivory and gold. It was obvious that clearing this chamber would prove even more difficult than the antechamber.

Carter was thinking ahead. The task in front of him was gigantic. He was going to need help, expert assistance and lots of supplies, especially chemicals and preservatives. He was also worried about security, in a country where tomb-robbing had been a traditional profession, the tomb was an obvious target. He decided that he must make immediate arrangements to fit an iron grille across the entrance to the tomb, in place of the plastered door they had removed that morning. It was clear that he had to go to Cairo. In the meantime, he could only place his most reliable guards at the entrance.

News of the discovery had spread, and as an act of diplomacy Carter thought it advisable to organize an official opening with local dignitaries present. The ceremony took place on November 29th and was attended by the Governor of the Province, the Mamour of the District, and other Egyptian officials and notables; Lady Allenby, Pierre Lacau the Director-General of the Service of Antiquities, and Mr. Merton correspondent of "The Times". It was Merton's story that really started the excitement in British newspapers, an excitement which was to reach the point of frenzy over the months and years that lay ahead.

On December 3rd the entrance to the tomb was again filled in, and on December 6th Carter left for Cairo to make all the necessary arrangements for the work that was to follow. His assistant, Callender, stayed behind to watch over the tomb, Lord Carnarvon and Lady Herbert having left for England two days earlier. They were to return later in the season.

The list of supplies was immense. Everything had to be anticipated well in advance. It was obvious to Carter that conservation was going to be a problem and they were going to need enormous amounts of packing materials and bandages. In all he purchased a mile of wadding, another mile of bandages, thirty-two bales of calico, chemicals, photographic materials, packing cases of all kinds, and last but not least a motor car.

By the 15th December everything had arrived in The Valley, including the steel gate. The Egyptian State Railway had given special permission for the supplies to travel by express rather than the usual freight train. By 18th December, the steel door was in position and they were ready to start work.

Their first task on entering the tomb was to make a thorough survey of the contents of the antechamber, only then could they begin to start removing the treasure. Carter had already realized that removing the many objects was going to prove difficult as a number were intricately entangled with their neighbours. Although they appeared strong, many were very weak and required strengthening and preserving before they could be moved, thus the first step was to make a preliminary list.

Immediately in front of the entrance was a beautiful semi-translucent alabaster wishing cup, the handles in the form of lotuses which supported two symbolic figures of Eternity. After gingerly stepping over this, they started to list the objects systematically as they went round the room. They had to be extremely careful, as one false move would have meant the destruction of an object which had lain undisturbed for all these years.

The first to attract their attention were two funerary bouquets of leaves which lay near a clutter of alabaster jars. Nearby was a painted wooden casket, an item of breathtaking beauty, it was the first real artistic masterpiece that Carter was able to examine closely. He was so enthralled that at the time he thought it would rank as the greatest artistic treasure in the tomb. The surface of the wooden casket was covered with a smooth layer of gesso, on which were painted the most superb scenes and designs in brilliant colour. On the side the young King was shown in battle and on the lid, hunting. The scenes on the ends were unusual, showing the King in the form of a lion, overcoming his enemies. These scenes depicting the King as a hunter and warrior were traditional, and in this case imaginary, as it is unlikely that Tutankhamun ever went to war. It was, however, thought necessary to suggest the warlike nature of the Pharaoh and Egypt's supremacy over her vassal states. The painting was so fine that it was impossible to see all the finer details without the aid of a magnifying glass. This box had a tremendous effect on Carter, who though appreciating the work as Egyptian, compared it mentally with the finest of Persian miniature paintings of recent times. He found it impossible to describe the fantastic beauty of the treasures. A problem still found today, for even the best colour photographs do not do the objects justice, one literally has to see to believe.

Ever so carefully Carter opened the box. To his surprise the contents were all a jumble, but when emptied there were revealed the Court robes of the King, garments never before found in an Egyptian tomb. When new they must have been truly impressive. They were covered with beadwork and gold sequins. One was covered with thousands of gold rosettes. Also included were three pairs of gold Court sandals and a gilt head-rest. In contrast on the very top of the box was a pair of rush sandals.

Carter's attention now turned to the three large animal-headed couches. They had been made in four pieces and were fitted together with hooks and staples. It was the first time actual examples had been found, before this their presence had only been hinted at by paintings on the walls of tombs. Each had the heads of a different animal fashioned in gilded wood. One had the heads of lions, the other of cows and the third of a composite animal, half crocodile and half hippopotamus.

The whole area, on, under and around the couches was crammed with objects. On one there was an oblong bed with an attractive carved panel and on this was a pile of objects including bows, quivers of arrows and staves. The bows were masterpieces of art. One had the ends fashioned in the form of captives, so designed that the string would form a noose around their necks

21

— a symbolic gesture ! The craftsmanship was superb.

On top of the couch were bronze and gold torch holders in the form of ankh — the sign of life, from which two arms projected to hold the torch, a type which had never been seen before. One even had the twisted linen still in the burner.

The effect of all this treasure on Carter and his assistants was overwhelming. It was like being involved in an adventure of the 1001 Nights and being magically transferred into Ali Baba's cave.

A casket of gold and faience of brilliant turquoise blue now caught their eye. This beautiful object was to yield further treasures when examined later in the laboratory. They did not know then that among its contents was a fantastic leopard skin ecclesiastical robe, decorated with gold and silver stars and a gilt leopard head. Such a robe is shown on a statue in the Museo Egizio, Turin, of Anen brother of Queen Tiye, who was priest of Heliopolis and Second Prophet of Amun.

Nearby, under the couch was a large chest of ivory, red wood and ebony. They opened it to find that it contained a number of alabaster vases. Also under the couch were shrines, an alabaster box of pigments and two folding stools in the form of ducks. A charming little child's chair was stacked close by. Made from ebony, gold and ivory, it was one of the relics of Tutankhamun's childhood.

Strewn throughout the antechamber were numerous boxes of all shapes and of all materials. One, made of black and white wood, stood in front of a couch. It contained a curious assortment of objects. On the bottom were staves, bows, and arrows, the latter with their points broken off, while on the top there was a jumble of the King's clothing. The staves were beautifully fashioned. One had its terminals in the form of a pair of realistically carved captives, one a negro, the other a Syrian. There was also a very fine ivory whip. Before turning his attention to the second couch, the one with cows' heads, Carter noticed a cluster of fine alabaster perfume jars and a toilet table.

The second couch also supported a bed, though this time painted white. On top of this was a rush work chair and another chair of red wood and ebony. Under the bed but on the couch, was an ivory and ebony veneered box and a white ornamented stool. Also on the couch were a pair of gilt sistra, an ancient musical instrument, rather like a rattle. The instrument is an attribute of the goddess Hathor often represented as a cow, cow-headed woman or a woman with a horned headdress. She is associated with love, joy and dancing, and known as the suckler of the King.

Beneath the couch they found offerings of food and a number of oval wooden cases. In front of the couch were two wooden boxes, one with a docket written in hieratic, a cursive form of hieroglyphics, (Egyptian picture writing) which listed the contents. The docket listed seventeen items of lapis lazuli blue, but when examined, the box contained only sixteen, all blue faience libation vases. The missing vase was found later in another part of the chamber. Apart from the vases, there were a number of other items of faience, electrum, ivory, etc., which had been thrown in rather carelessly. There was also a fragment of a rather intriguing corselet and a garment of elaborate tapestry. Two fine electrum boomerangs also attracted their attention. Nearby on its side was an exquisite carved cedarwood chair, finely worked and decorated with gold.

Hardly able to comprehend all that they had seen, they turned their attention to the third couch. This couch, like the others, was decorated with the heads of animals but in this case they were composite animals, half crocodile, half hippopotamus, open mouthed with ivory tongues and teeth. On the top of the couch was a solitary chest. It had an ebony frame with white painted panels and rounded top. When Carter had first entered the tomb, he had peered into this chest and had mistakenly thought that it contained papyri, documents written on rolls of paper made from the papyrus reed. Now, when they examined the chest again, it was clear that it contained not rolls of papyri but the King's underlinen, rolled into bundles. Before they knew this, Carter's mistake attracted a great deal of excitement in the press when the news of the discovery first broke.

Sir Ernest Budge, a well known Egyptologist, wrote in "The Times" of December 1st 1922, "Our curiosity is whetted by the mention of the box containing rolls of papyri, mentioned in the despatch in "The Times", and we hope that Lord Carnarvon will at once take steps to have them unrolled and examined".

On December 9th it had been announced also in "The Times", that "Dr. Alan Gardiner will accept the invitation of Mr. Howard Carter to undertake the philogical work in connection with the papyri found in the antechamber of the Tomb".

As so often happens, first impressions turn out to be wrong and all the speculation caused by the so-called papyri was to no avail. However, Gardiner did join Carter, for there was much for him to do, with the inscriptions that covered many objects.

Beneath the couch was another treasure of breath-taking beauty, the marvellous throne of Tutankhamun. It was covered in gold from top to bottom and was encrusted with coloured stones, faience, and glass. The arms were in the form of magnificent winged and crowned serpents supporting the cartouche of the King.

The legs were in the form of lion's legs, the front two supporting two beautifully carved lions' heads. Between the seat and the stretchers that connected the four legs, there were originally panels, probably in open-work, but these were now missing. The back was so fantastically beautiful that Carter had no hesitation in describing it, in 1923, as the most beautiful thing that had yet been found in Egypt. It has since been illustrated so many times, both in colour and black and white, that it must surely be one of the most familiar works of Egyptian art. The scene represented is that of the young King in profile, seated informally on a throne facing his Queen Ankhesenamun, who is affectionately anointing his shoulders with scented oil. The composition in the Amarna tradition is among the most charming in Egyptian art. The King and Queen are depicted with realism and the colourings are exquisite. The girlish figure of the Queen is beautifully portrayed with the many pleats of her robe accentuating the outline of her body, but for all her feminine charm, it is evident that she is but a young girl. The King too is shown as a youth in his teens. The whole scene pulsates with life, and the colours of the inlays of glass, faience, cornelian and other stones blend to create a vivid effect, when combined with the gold and silver. Although the gold and silver has dulled over the centuries, when fresh the effect must have been brilliant.

The throne is in pure Amarna style, the artistic tradition developed under the so-called heretic king, Akhenaten. Above the throne is the sun-disc, Aten, with its rayed hands extending downwards towards the young couple. It is obvious that the chair was made when the worship of Aten was still practised, or when it had not completely fallen into disfavour. However, changes had been made to the chair and in places the name of Aten had been replaced with Amun, although this was not general and the name of Aten still remained in places. Carter thought it curious that such a symbol of the worship of Aten should be placed in a tomb so strongly and obviously connected with Amun, and suggested that it may have been too valuable an object to discard, or that perhaps the King had paid only lip service to the worship of Amun. The truth will probably never be known but there are one or two peculiarities that need pointing out. The worship of Aten was supposed to have fallen into disfavour, towards the end of the reign of Akhenaten. The figure of Tutankhamun as portrayed on the back of the throne, suggests that he was at least fourteen when it was made. This leads us to the possibility that five years after the death of Akhenaten, objects decorated with the sun-disc Aten were still being made. In order for the chair to have been made during the reign of Akhenaten, Tutankhamun would have had to have been about eight to nine years old, and Ankhesenamun to be about nine to ten. The ages of the couple on the back of the throne certainly appear to be greater than this. Another unanswered question is why weren't all the names of Aten removed? It appears as if the job was never finished. This is very strange as there would have been ample time for the necessary changes to have been made during Tutankhamun's reign. The missing panels between the stretchers and the seat are also intriguing. It has been suggested that they were wrenched from position by tomb robbers, but this also seems strange when there must have been many more valuable and portable objects in the tomb which could have been taken. Could it be possible that these panels were removed, and the changes made at a later date, after the King had been entombed?

On the throne rested the footstool which had

26

originally stood in front. Nearby, in front of the couch were two other stools, one of ebony and ivory, and the other of painted wood.

With great effort they managed to tear their attention away from the throne and concentrate once more on the numerous other treasures that littered the tomb. Against the south wall of the chamber was a shrine-box, entirely covered with thick sheet gold, on which were embossed in low relief touching scenes of the everyday life of the King. Another fine example of the art of the school of Amarna, here too, the names of Aten had been replaced with those of Amun. The shrine may have originally contained a gold figure but it was one of the objects taken by tomb robbers, and all that was left inside was the pedestal, a quantity of jewellery, and another part of the corselet which they had found elsewhere. At the side of the shrine was a carved and gilded shawbati figure of the King. These figures were intended to act as deputies for the deceased in the next world and perform whatever manual work was required. Next to the shawbati was an unusual life size painted wooden statue of the King, with no arms, and with the figure ending at the waist. A fascinating object, it was probably the King's mannequin used for fitting his robes.

The whole of the east wall and part of the south wall was littered with a mass of chariot parts, which when later sorted out and assembled, turned out to be the components of four vehicles. Although in disarray due to the plundering of the tomb, their condition was in part due to the fact that they were too big to carry into the tomb and had to be sawn into a number of pieces.

By the time the survey was finished, and Carter had checked his notes, he found that there were at least six to seven hundred objects in the antechamber. He now knew that his task would be gigantic.

CHAPTER THREE

★

PROBLEMS

By the time they were ready to clear the antechamber, Carter had assembled his team. Extensive and immediate help had been offered by the Metropolitan Museum of Art, New York, at a time when Carnarvon and Carter were getting anxious about the size of the operation that lay ahead. The Curator of the Egyptian Department of the Metropolitan Museum, Mr. A. M. Lythgoe, had offered the assistance of the Museum's own expedition in Egypt, and consequently Carter obtained the services of Harry Burton, a gifted photographer; Messrs. Hall and Houser, draughtsmen; and Mr. A. C. Mace, the Assistant Curator of the Metropolitan Museum, and Director of the Museum's excavations in the pyramid field at Lisht. Further assistance came from Mr. Lucas, Director of the Chemical Department of the Egyptian Government, who offered his services to the excavation prior to his retirement. During the work that was to follow, further help and advice was given by Dr. Alan Gardiner and Professor Breasted.

Gradually the company assembled and work began on clearing the antechamber. Hall and Houser concentrated on making a plan of the antechamber, while Burton began experiments to determine the best method of photographing the treasure. Lucas established his laboratory and began work experimenting with methods of preserving the objects. On the 27th December the first object was removed from the tomb.

Clearing the antechamber proved to be like a large child's game of spillikins, but one in which the stakes were very high. The chamber was so crowded that an elaborate system of props and buttresses had to be developed, in order to ensure that in moving one object, dozens of others did not tumble to the ground. Many items which looked strong and robust, would, if not treated with the utmost care, disintegrate on being touched. Lucas' job was immense, for there were numerous objects that had to be treated then and there, before they could be moved. They then required further work in the laboratory before they could be transported.

Everything had to be well planned and conducted systematically. It was decided that Burton would first photograph the objects, which previously had numbers arranged in front of them, and then Hall and Houser would place the objects on their scale plan. Carter and Callender concentrated on the clearing of the chamber and superintending the transport of the treasure to the laboratory, where Lucas and Mace would carry out the detailed process of examination, repair and preservation. Burton, through the kind permission of the Egyptian Government, had established a dark room in an empty tomb which was close by. It was ironical that this tomb should have been that which Theodore Davis had discovered some years previously, and which he had called the cache tomb of Akhenaten. This tomb will figure prominently later in our story.

It was essential for Burton to be able to process his photographs without delay, so that when experimenting with exposures, he could make a mad dash from the tomb to his dark room to see the results, before moving his equipment. With the great interest in the excavation, he usually had an audience of visitors who were thrilled at the sight of his constant sprints back and forth. Lucas, on the other hand, was installed in seclusion in another tomb, that of Seti II, at the other end of The Valley in an area which was not normally visited by tourists and therefore would not attract as much attention. This suited Carter down to the ground, as one of his great problems was to ensure the security of objects being preserved in the laboratory. The path leading to the laboratory was sealed off, and in the evening when the work was finished, a large steel gate weighing one and a half tons, was fitted in position and secured by numerous padlocks. Although this tomb was rather restrictive in size, the disadvantages were outweighed by the comparative privacy and reasonable stability of the atmosphere. It was well sheltered by overhanging cliffs and remained cool even in the hottest weather.

When we realize that this operation was taking place virtually in the middle of nowhere, five hundred miles from Cairo, we can imagine the difficulties they encountered in maintaining supplies. Several times they exhausted the entire Cairo stock of certain chemicals and it was necessary to plan well in advance to ensure that work should not be held up.

One of the difficulties in recording the position of each object, was that there were many that could not be seen or discovered, until others that were hiding them were removed. Even with systematic numbering, the exact relationship between objects would not always be apparent. Carter solved this problem by having numerous photographs taken of groups of objects, each one individually numbered, and during each stage of clearing, so that when the notes were written up they could be filed with a photograph of the object, showing its relationship with other items.

All Burton's photography in the antechamber was carried out with the aid of two stands of bulbs, giving an even spread of light of about 3,000 candle power. Some exposures took a little time, but today we can be thankful to Burton for his mastery over the difficult conditions and for the superb record he has left behind.

Carter's fascination for the painted box with hunting and battle scenes of Tutankhamun, must have prompted him to remove it without delay, and in fact it was the first object that he removed from the tomb. In all it took seven weeks to clear the antechamber. Seven weeks during which time their nerves must have been stretched almost to breaking point. Certainly by the end of this period, Carter notes with relief that they had removed everything without mishap, no easy task. Although Carter was criticised many times throughout the operation for the length of time that he took to clear the tomb — others were anxious for quick results — it really is a fantastic piece of work to record, clear and preserve over seven hundred objects in seven weeks.

Throughout the operation Howard Carter was conscious of his great responsibility, not only to his patron, Lord Carnarvon in particular, but to archaeology and society in general. He felt privileged to be entrusted with the task of the recording and removal of the treasure, and was ever conscious of the danger of laziness, slackness, or the haste of curiosity. He wrote in the first volume of "The Tomb of Tutankhamen".

"Destruction of evidence is so painfully easy — yet so hopelessly irreparable . . . . It had been our privilege to find the most important collection of Egyptian antiquities that had ever seen the light, and it was for us to show that we were worthy of the trust. So many things there were that might go wrong."*

Everyone was working flat out, but perhaps apart from the great weight of responsibility on Carter's shoulders, the greatest burden fell on Lucas, who had to deal with the enormous task of the preservation of

31

objects, for which no standard method of treatment was known. Many a time he would have to treat an object in position, either by melted paraffin wax, as in the case of a pair of beaded sandals, which although perfect to look at were in fact a mass of individual beads, the thread having decayed centuries earlier; or as, in the case of the funerary bouquets, sprayed with liquid celluloid before they could be moved. We can be thankful for his foresight, for if the preservation had been entrusted to someone less conscientious, numerous objects would not have survived.

While many of the smaller items presented problems of preservation before handling, the larger objects, namely the three large couches and the chariots, presented problems of a different nature, due to their very size. The couches were made in four parts, the two sides in the shape of animals, the base to which the animal's feet were attached, and the couch support. It was obvious that they had originally been brought into the tomb in pieces and assembled during the funeral. Carter found, however, that taking them apart would not be as easy as he had hoped, the entrance passage being far too narrow for them to be taken out whole, therefore, the only way was as they had come in, in sections. Taking them apart was not an easy matter, and try as they might, they could not move the bronze hooks that were tightly wedged in the staples. Eventually they succeeded, but it took five men to do it. But their troubles were not yet over, for manoeuvring the animal sides through the tomb was no easy matter. However, they were lucky and managed to remove all three without damage. The chariots proved more difficult than the couches. It was obvious that they had presented great difficulty to the funerary party in the first instance, as they were far too large to negotiate the entrance passage and had to have the axles sawn off, in order to get them into the tomb. They were very lightly made and the harsh treatment that they had endured made them difficult to handle. Another problem was caused by the fact that most of the leather harnesses, which were made of undressed leather, had decomposed, turning into a black glutinous mass, which had run and dripped not only on the chariots, but on to other objects near them. Such were the many difficulties posed by the objects themselves.

There were other problems too, the security of the whole operation was extremely difficult. The publicity had been widespread both in Egypt and throughout the world, and there was every possibility of a large scale raid on the tomb. Realizing this, Carter organised an ingenious system of guarding the tomb, a system that will be readily appreciated by anyone who has worked in the Middle East. He split his guards into three groups, each group responsible to a different authority and each watch made up of all three groups. Each group to watch the other ! There was a guard from the Department of Antiquities, a guard from the most trustworthy of his own staff, and a squad of soldiers seconded by the Mudir of Kewa. The massive steel gate at the inner entrance to the tomb and the heavy wooden grille at the entrance to the passage, were each fastened with four padlocked chains, the keys of which were entrusted to a senior member of his team.

By the middle of February, the antechamber had been cleared. It had been carefully swept many times and all the crevices carefully inspected, to ensure that nothing escaped their notice. With the exception of the two sentinel figures of the King, the antechamber was empty and they were ready to turn their attention to opening the sealed door.

* Howard Carter and A. C. Mace "The Tomb of Tut-Ankh-Amen" Cassell, London, 1923.

CHAPTER FOUR

★

SPLENDOUR

It was Friday 17th February 1923. A group of high ranking and learned spectators had gathered in the now cleared antechamber to watch the opening of the sealed doorway, a drama that had never been seen before or is likely to be seen again. Everyone was keyed up. The atmosphere was electric. Everyone, not least Carter, wondered what lay in store. Over four months had passed since they had first entered the tomb, now they were at last to see what lay behind the seals. The tomb had been international news for months and amongst the party that waited to peer into the sealed chamber were experts from Britain and America; the Egyptologist Dr. Alan Gardiner, Professor Breasted, Mr. Lythgoe, Curator of the Egyptian Department, Metropolitan Museum of Art, New York, M. Lacau, Director General of the Service of Antiquities, and Mr. Engelbach, Chief Inspector of the Department, together with three of his associates, Lord Carnarvon and his daughter Lady Evelyn Herbert, H. E. Abdl el Halim Pasha Suleman, Minister of Public Works, a few other important spectators and a representative of the Government Press Bureau, in all about twenty. All waited anxiously for the wonders that must surely appear.

In the careful and scientific clearing of the antechamber, Carter and his colleagues had been enthralled and absorbed by the riches and quality of the treasure they examined. The wonder and fascination that they had known during those arduous months was to be repeated. With the antechamber completely clear except for the two black and gold sentinel figures, they turned their attention to the mysterious sealed doorway that these two figures, in the likeness of the King, armed with mace and staff, had guarded for so long. All present must have made their own personal guess as to what would be found when this door, that had been tantalising them for months, was demolished. Where was the mummy of the King, so conspicuous by its absence ? Would they have the good fortune to find it or was this doorway hiding the anticlimax to their hard work ?

The antechamber was rather like a theatre, with the chairs that had been prepared for the visitors arranged in a line facing the sealed doorway. The statues of the King had been boarded to protect them, and a small platform had been prepared to enable them to reach the lintel, where they would start their operation. It was to be a matinée performance, as it was 2-15 in the afternoon when the operations began. The scene must have been quite bizarre, the battery of lamps on either side throwing weird shadows against the walls. With butterflies in his stomach and with trembling hands, Carter struck the first blow, and carefully chipped away the plaster around the lintel. Gradually, as he chipped away the small stones on the top layer, a small hole appeared. He admitted later that the temptation to stop every now and then to peer inside was irresistible, but it wasn't until he had worked for about ten minutes that there was a hole big enough to insert an electric torch. Prepared as he was by what he had seen in the antechamber, he was still astonished at what he saw. There before him was what appeared to be a solid wall of gold.

His excitement seemed to flow into the audience, who were gripped by the drama of the moment. No Hitchcock film could even approach the suspense that was being created. As excited as Carter was, he realized that his job was extremely dangerous, and that one false move would send a block of stone crashing into the inner-chamber, and shattering the treasure that had lain undisturbed for centuries.

The whole operation was beset with difficulties, the blocks were not uniform in size and were extremely heavy. Carter found that he could not successfully remove the doorway alone, so he sought the help of Mace and Callender. He would gently ease up a stone, Mace would grip it to prevent it falling forwards into the chamber, and then lift it off and pass it to Callender, who would pass it by a chain of workmen out of the tomb. After a time it became clear that the solid wall of gold was in fact a gigantic golden shrine, which almost entirely filled the chamber. Gradually, stone by stone, the doorway was removed and two hours later they were able to enter the chamber. A sense of awe enveloped them. What they saw before them was infinitely more beautiful than anything they'd seen before. They must have whispered reverently, as they sensed they were in the presence of the King.

The chamber was at a lower level than the ante-chamber, and it proved very difficult to enter, although fortunately, there were no objects in front of them to bar their passage. Cautiously edging his way round the shrine, Carter was able to see to the end of the chamber. There was almost a clear passage, except for a pair of most magnificent alabaster vases, superior to any that he had seen in the antechamber. Realizing that these were the only objects that barred his way to the end of the chamber, he carefully marked their position and passed them back to the party in the antechamber.

Edging his way forward in the narrow passage between the shrine and the walls of the chamber, he was amazed by the gigantic size of the shrine. It was so enormous, that it almost filled the entire area of the chamber, leaving only a narrow space, about two feet wide in between, while the top of the shrine almost reached the ceiling. Afterwards they found that it in fact measured 17 feet x 11 feet x 9 feet high, the entire shrine covered in gold on which various magical symbols were inlaid in blue faience. Carter was now joined by Lord Carnarvon and M. Lacau and together they edged their way to the far end of the chamber. By now their hearts must have been beating almost uncontrollably. They could see the superb splendour of the shrine and yet all the time they wondered, had the tomb robbers violated it and plundered the mummy of the King ? Their questions were soon to be answered, for at the east end they came upon the great folding doors, they were closed and bolted, but not sealed. Their hearts sank.

Overcoming this disappointment, their hopes rose as they realized there would be other shrines within. They remembered a papyrus dating to the time of Ramesses IV that mentioned that there were normally at least four shrines, and there was always a chance that one of these would be sealed and the mummy intact. Their curiosity fired once more, they drew back the bolt and swung open the doors of the outer shrine. There before them was the answer to all their prayers, a door with its seals intact, and within, the first unplundered burial of an Egyptian King. Although their instincts were to break the seal, they knew that they could not do this for risk of destroying the shrine, and so they decided to leave the investigation of the interior to a later date.

After closing the doors of the shrine, they made their way to the eastern end of the chamber where they discovered something they had not anticipated. There was another doorway! Unlike the others, it was not sealed and they were able to see clearly inside. It is difficult for us to imagine today what their feelings must have been. The feeling of euphoria must have been infinitely greater than that obtained by winning the Pools. Let us try to put ourselves in their position. Imagine first your discovery of the tomb itself some months previously, then that day, discovering not only the superb gilded shrine, with its inner sealed doors protecting the untouched body of Tutankhamun, but on top of this finding another chamber full of treasure. Even from where they stood, they could easily tell that this little room held objects of far greater beauty than any they had seen in the antechamber. The glint of gold was everywhere.

Moving into the room, Carter's attention was at once attracted by an object of indescribable beauty. It affected him in much the same way as had the painted box in the antechamber, but even more so. It was a shrine surrounded by a group of four tutelary goddesses of the dead. The figures were so beautiful, graceful, and their expressions so compassionate, that he felt it almost sacrilege to look at them. These figures stood at each corner of a large golden shrine, surmounted by a cornice of sacred cobras. It was the "Canopic" chest with the jars containing the viscera of the dead King.

For a moment they could not take their eyes off this wonderful chest with its four guardian goddesses, but slowly they began to notice other treasures in the room. First they noticed a figure of the jackal god Anubis which lay at the entrance to the chamber, then close behind, the head of a bull on a stand both symbols of the Nether World. Now and then their eyes would flit back to the wonderful figures of the goddesses, then they would notice other objects. Shrines, chests, most of them sealed, one that was not, contained a superb figure of the King standing on black leopards. There were numerous shrine-boxes and miniature gilded wooden coffins. In the centre of the chamber, all in a row, were a number of beautiful ivory and wood caskets, inlaid with blue faience and gold. Carter lifted the lid of one to find a fabulous ostrich feather fan, apparently as fresh as the day it was made. Around the room at various points were models of ships with sails and rigging. Opposite the shrines and chests that lined one side of the wall, was a superb chariot. Unlike the antechamber here everything was in order, and there appeared little evidence of disturbance. Everything still remained as it was at the time of burial. Hardly able to take it all in, Carter and Carnarvon edged their way back into the antechamber to allow the others to see the fantastic sight. As the passage was so narrow, Carter only allowed the visitors into the burial chamber in two's and three's. Each emerged from the chamber with dazzled eyes. Most said nothing, speechless from what they had seen. Others found that words could not adequately express their thoughts, what they had seen was beyond description. The party emerged from the tomb late that afternoon in a dazed condition, in some way changed by their experience — they had travelled time itself.

CHAPTER FIVE

★

BURIAL

A week after they had entered the burial chamber, Carter again closed the tomb. Then followed a series of unfortunate events, not least the death of Lord Carnarvon from pneumonia, in April 1923. The Countess of Carnarvon decided that the work on the tomb should continue, in memory of her husband, and negotiated with the Department of Antiquities for the enterprise to continue until November 1st 1924. Even allowing for the death of Lord Carnarvon, which must have had a dampening effect on the members of the excavation, the atmosphere was not as happy as it could be considering the marvellous task at hand. Relations were strained between Carter, the Press, and the Egyptian Government, and he was afraid that if the number of so-called official visits continued to grow at the same rate as in the past, he would find it almost impossible to do any serious work. With this on his mind, he arrived in Cairo on October 8th 1923 to carry on, determined to avoid friction if he could.

He had already decided that the second season's work should concentrate on the burial chamber, and he realized that the only way he was going to be able to work safely in the chamber, was to remove the partition wall between the antechamber and the burial chamber. Before he could do this he had to remove the two life size wooden figures of the King, which had guarded the entrance to the burial chamber so well over the centuries. They were carefully wrapped, packed and removed from the tomb. When demolished, the wall that was covered on both sides with plaster, turned out to be constructed from dry masonry held together by logs of wood. Before he could turn his attention to the marvellous golden shrine, he had to remove the many objects that were packed between the walls of the burial chamber and perimeter of the shrine. One of the most beautiful and intriguing objects was a superb translucent alabaster lamp, resting on a trelliswork pedestal. Each side of the lamp was an alabaster fretwork panel symbolising eternal life and unity and bearing the cartouche of Tutankhamun. The intriguing aspect of this lamp is that when lit, an image of the King and Queen in brilliant colours appears on the front of the lamp, while on the back the names of Tutankhamun appear between garlands of floral ornament. At first it was not clear how this was achieved, but later Carter found that this ingenious effect had been created by turning the bowl of the lamp in two parts, painting the names and scenes on the inner bowl and then enclosing it in the outer bowl, so that when not lit they could not be seen.

Near the lamp was a fine silver trumpet, which apart from its tarnished condition was almost as fine as the day it was made. Recently, in a programme broadcast by the B.B.C., this trumpet was blown as it must have been during the funeral ceremony, although it was probably a military trumpet. In front of the doors of the golden shrine, which protected the sarcophagus of Tutankhamun, stood an exquisite lotus-form lamp in translucent alabaster, perhaps symbolising the Theban triad. Standing in front of the eastern wall near the lamp was the sacred goose of Amun, the wooden figure varnished black and wrapped in linen. At its side was a wine jar with the inscription, "Year 5, wine of the house of Tutankhamun from the Western River chief of the vintners, Kha", and two rush baskets in a collapsed condition. Along the western wall were ten magic oars of wood, placed there to ferry the King's boat across the waters of the Nether World. At each end of this narrow passage, between the walls of the burial chamber and the shrine, were queer wooden objects heavily varnished with black resin. One was a vase and the other two were wooden cubicles containing blue faience cups, one filled with natron and the other resin.   As one might expect in a tomb there were numerous reminders of the Nether World. At the north-west and north-east corners of the chamber stood two golden emblems of the jackal god Anubis, probably placed there to guide the deceased through the Nether World. Near to them were four curious gilt wooden objects and beside them four small rough clay troughs. The peculiar customs connected with the burial rites are so remote from us today, that it would be almost impossible to guess the exact significance of these objects. In the south-west corner was a massive olive and persea bouquet.

When the last of these had been removed to the laboratory, Carter was able to begin tackling the gigantic task of dismantling and removing the golden shrine. When we look back today, we can see that the scaffolding and hoisting tackle that he erected was extremely primitive, and it must have been a very difficult and hazardous job indeed, to dismantle the shrine without damage to it or to members of the party. The scaffolding in position, he began by unhinging the large doors of the outer shrine. The doors were hinged on copper pivots and to remove them the entablature had to be raised to release the upper and lower pivots. The roof was then hoisted off in three sections, after which the four sections of the entablature were removed. The operation of removing the shrines was extremely tedious and arduous and took in all eighty four days, most of them interrupted by visits from officials and others.

The entablature removed, the panels of the shrine, which was now almost only supported by the temporary struts which Carter had erected, could now be eased from the four corner uprights. They found it was impossible to remove them from the chamber, Carter therefore had to lean them against the walls of the burial chamber, until all the shrines had been dismantled. This operation was extremely difficult in such a confined space, and we must remember that the temperature in the tomb must have been very high indeed. The panels of the shrine too, were no light weight, being made of $2\frac{1}{4}$ inch oak planking covered in sheet gold, each weighing between $\frac{1}{4}$ and $\frac{3}{4}$ of a ton. Throughout the operation Carter was conscious of the fact that the shrine could damage so easily. The wood had shrunk over the three thousand three hundred years it had stood in the dry atmosphere of the tomb, though it was still in perfect condition. This had the effect of causing a gap between the gold work and the wood, which could cause the ornamental gold surface to crush if touched. Another problem was that the shrines were held together by tongues, the position and arrangement of which had been purposely secreted by the Egyptian craftsmen. Carter found that he could only discover their positions by tracing the minute cracks between the different sections, and then inserting a fine saw and severing them. More than once he thought he had discovered the positions of the tongues, only to find that in the next shrine, they had been arranged in a different way. Sometimes there were hidden tongues of solid bronze bearing the name of Tutankhamun, these of course could not be sawn through and had to be treated in a different way.

43

Before they could safely work on the shrines, a number of objects that were packed between the first outer shrine and the inner shrine had to be removed, including a superb alabaster perfume vase embellished with gold and ivory. This elaborate vase was constructed in four parts. The vase itself stood on an openwork stand on which two solar hawks supported the King's cartouche with their wings. On either side of the vase was a figure of the goddess Hapi, the surrounding openwork ornament symbolising the union of Upper and Lower Egypt. Nearby stood another superb cosmetic jar, this time cylindrical, the body decorated with hunting scenes, engraved and filled with coloured pigments, supported on prisoners' heads of black and red hardstones. At two sides were lotus columns. The lid revolved, the hinge and knobs being of red coloured ivory. On the top was a recumbent lion with the cartouche of Tutankhamun. This little treasure is unique, embodying elements of Eastern Mediterranean artistic ideals. It seemed almost that the finest objects were reserved for sealing in the space between the various shrines. In the corners were stacks of ceremonial sticks, staves, batons, maces and bows. Some of these were absolutely wonderful, their beauty almost impossible to describe. Sometimes they were surmounted by tiny metal figures of the young King, representing him at a very early age. The batons were exquisite, elaborately decorated in minute marquetry of various coloured woods, ivory, and iridescent wings of beetles. Not all of them were elaborate, there was a simple gold stick with a lapis lazuli glass top inscribed, "take for thyself the wand of gold, in order that thou mayest follow thy beloved father Amun, most beloved of the gods". Another stick was inscribed "the beautiful stick of His Majesty". Also among the sticks was a very simple one, an ordinary plain reed, but richly mounted. Carter wondered why such an ordinary reed should be so elegantly mounted, and then read the touching inscription which explained it all, "a reed which His Majesty cut with his own hand".

The alabaster perfume pots were covered with part of a linen pall that completely covered the second shrine, but which had begun to disintegrate. After the pall had been treated with a special solution, it was able to be rolled up and they saw the second shrine in its entirety for the first time. It was very similar to the first, the main difference being that it did not have the blue faience inlay. The doors were bolted on the top and the bottom and sealed with two impressions, one being the name of Tutankhamun over a "jackal and nine captives" and the other the seal of the royal necropolis the "jackal and nine captives", without any other mark.

Carter's heart was now thumping like a steam hammer, as he cut the cords, removed the seals and opened the door of the second shrine. Scarcely daring to breathe, he looked inside to find yet a third shrine, sealed like the second. It was one of the rare occasions when Carter gave in to curiosity. Where normally he would plod methodically along, removing objects, recording them, removing more objects, recording them, he now realized that he could if he wanted, break the seals of the shrine and open the inner doors, to look upon that which no man had seen since it was closed, nearly thirty-three centuries before by the priests of the royal necropolis. Behind these doors Carter was sure lay the undisturbed body of the young King, to whom he was now so close in many ways, in spite of the large expanse of time. Time itself seemed to have disappeared. He gave in, and with carefully disguised excitement cut the cord, removed the seals, and opened the doors. There before his eyes was a golden shrine even more beautiful than the last. Behind it he knew must lie the sarcophagus of the Golden

Monarch. By this time, almost in a daze by what he had seen, and in anticipation of what he was about to see, he drew back the doors of the fourth shrine, and gazed at last upon a vast yellow quartzite sarcophagus. It was a fantastic moment for Howard Carter. The culmination of all the years of toil, and the anticipation of months during the careful clearing of the antechamber. The sarcophagus entirely filled the area enclosed by the shrine. Its lid lay in place, as it had been left centuries earlier when it had been fixed in position. At each corner of the sarcophagus was a goddess, Isis, Nephthys, Neith and Selkit, whose outstretched wings and hands guarded the King from intruders. Having thus satisfied his curiosity, he sobered up and over the next month concentrated on removing the other shrines.

Like the space between the first and second shrines, the space between the third and fourth was also stacked with objects. Ceremonial bows and arrows, and fans, the important emblems of State, one of which had a fine portrait of the young King in his chariot, accompanied by a hound, embossed on the gold surface. The reverse showed him returning from the chase complete with his kill, two ostriches, whose feathers were no doubt intended for the fan. The handle was inscribed "the Eastern Desert of Heliopolis". Another, bearing the cartouches of Tutankhamun, and encrusted with turquoise, lapis lazuli and cornelian, was also inscribed "life to the beautiful ruler". The plumes of the fans had completely disintegrated due to the activity of insects, but sufficient remained to show that each fan had forty two plumes, arranged alternately white and brown.

The innermost shrine (fourth) proved quite a problem for Carter, for he was surprised to find that the roof and cornice were different to the others and were made in a single piece. It turned out to be one of his most difficult problems. It was extremely heavy and took several days of hard labour before it eventually could be removed and taken into the antechamber. This done, the four sides of the last shrine were removed, and the work of over eighty days completed. The sarcophagus now stood resplendent in the centre of the room, freed from its golden shields. It was a magnificent piece of work, carved from a solid block of yellow quartzite. It was 9 feet in length, 4 feet 10 inches wide and 4 feet 10 inches high. Even allowing for the numerous other sarcophagi that have been found in Egypt, there is no doubt that it is one of the finest. Carter was greatly affected, standing as he did in the presence of the King. No doubt his thoughts went back to the time of the King's burial, with all the pomp and ceremony that must have surrounded the interment of the young Monarch. Although the sarcophagus itself was in perfect condition, the lid which was of rose granite, was cracked in the middle. The cracks had been cemented and carefully painted in an attempt to disguise them. This unusual feature suggested to Carter that some accident had befallen the original quartzite lid, and as time may have been extremely short the granite lid which was itself imperfect, had been substituted.

Again ceremony and diplomacy intervened and interrupted the work. Etiquette demanded that a large number of officials and various interested parties would have to be present when the lid was removed. And so on the appointed day a most bizarre scene was enacted in the burial chamber, with not only officials from the Egyptian Government present, but Egyptologists from Britain, France and America. Practically everyone who thought they should be there, was there. The atmosphere was electric with anticipation. The speculations of years were about to be answered.

The crack in the lid made its removal more difficult than if it had been intact. A system of scaffolding and differential pulleys had been erected, for it was hoped to raise it in one piece. Eventually, by inserting angle irons along the side of the slab, the lid, weighing over $1\frac{1}{4}$ tons, rose and the light of the twentieth century shone into the sarcophagus, which had sealed the King in darkness for all those centuries. When light filled the sarcophagus the party had something of an anticlimax, for whatever they were expecting to see they did not. The contents were entirely covered by linen shrouds. So with suspense still in the air, Carter pulled back the shrouds to reveal a sight so wonderful that it caused everyone, including Carter, to gasp with admiration. There before them was a most magnificent golden effigy of the King, filling the entire sarcophagus. This was obviously the large golden outermost coffin which promised even further wondrous sights within.

The coffin, which measured about 7 feet in length rested on a bier, fashioned in the shape of a lion. The gold body of the King was protected by two fantastic golden figures of the goddesses, Isis and Neith. The King was shown mummified, his hands arranged across his chest, holding the crook and flail, the royal emblems Everywhere was brilliant gold, with the exception of the inlays. The face had eyes of argonite and obsidian, and eyelids and eyebrows inlaid with lapis lazuli glass. The makers had achieved a clever effect of realism, by fashioning the face and hands in a different alloy of sheet gold, thereby accentuating them from the golden mummified body. The effect was of the realism of death. The emblems of Upper and Lower Egypt, the cobra and vulture, were emblazoned on the King's forehead. Here then was the Golden Monarch, lying in the stillness of death, surrounded everywhere by a ransom of gold, yet the whole occasion humanised by a touching gesture from his young Queen, Ankhesenamun, who had placed a small wreath of flowers on the body of her young husband, as a touching symbol of farewell. The flowers still retained their colours, reminding us how short time really is. The audience that day experienced more than that which they had seen with their eyes. They felt something of the events of long ago. After the party had gone, the King was left resplendent in his golden coffins. For between now and the time that he and Howard Carter would come face to face, would be months of twentieth century diplomatic and political frustrations which Carter would have to endure. He did not know it at the time, but it was not to be until the end of 1925 that he would be able to resume his work on the coffins.

CHAPTER SIX

★

DISPUTE

Ever since the discovery of the tomb, public interest had been growing at a fantastic rate. The overwhelming reportage in the world's press resulted in numerous requests for news and interviews from newspapers large and small. It was obvious to Lord Carnarvon, at the very beginning, that they would not be able to handle the press coverage, and he had therefore made an agreement with "The Times" for them to handle the entire news coverage. This may have been satisfactory to Carnarvon, but it was certainly not satisfactory to the world's press, who were continually bickering amongst themselves to get exclusive interviews and news. The regurgitation of news through another newspaper simply did not appeal to them. Neither did it appeal to the Egyptian Government, which felt that Lord Carnarvon was taking a little too much upon himself. Lord Carnarvon, on the other hand, felt quite justified in making the agreement, as he was under the impression that the concession he held from the Egyptian Government, allowed him to have sole rights of publication. As time went by things got worse and not better. It was almost a case of world interest becoming so great as to threaten the excavation itself.

As a result of the publicity in the press, there were

hoards of visitors to The Valley of the Kings, all who came daily, reserved their seats and sat hoping to see something of the work being carried on in the tomb. All would install themselves complete with sun-hats or shades, a book, knitting, and the inevitable camera. Everything that moved was photographed. Sometimes the click click click click click, sounded more like the castanets in a Spanish tavern than the middle of the Egyptian desert. Indeed, one piece of mummy cloth that was required for some laboratory experiments, was photographed no less than eight times during its journey through The Valley. Carter took all this good humouredly, but when it came to the numerous requests from officialdom to visit the tomb, and the many attempts by others with no official connection or excuse, but who would go to any end to enter the tomb, this became too much. In fact it became almost impossible to carry out any archaeological work whatsoever. Add to this the increasing red-tape and suspicion, that was being built up between the excavators and the Egyptian Government, then we can see that the situation was reaching crisis point. The Egyptian Government were worried about the terms of their agreement, which were on the whole rather vague, and were naturally anxious to ensure that none of the treasures left Egypt. On the other hand, Lord Carnarvon had invested a great deal of money in the expedition and would naturally assume that he was entitled to some of the objects as compensation, something that Carter adamantly opposed. In fact it grew into almost a feud between the two men.

Even within a few weeks of the discovery of the tomb one could see that the seeds of this feud had already been sown.

Sir Ernest Budge fired the first salvo in an article in "The Times" published December 1st, 1922. He wrote,

"The laws which govern excavations made by foreigners in Egypt, used to allot to the excavator one half of the 'find.' Under Maspero, (the previous Director of Antiquities) these laws were interpreted generously, and one must hope that such will be the case in respect of the present discovery."

A few days later on December 4th, Alan Gardiner wrote in "The Times",

"One cannot help hoping that Lord Carnarvon who has worked for so many years in Egypt without any adequate compensation for all his efforts, will be able to bring home what is not absolutely essential to the Cairo Museum."

The feud ended with the death of Lord Carnarvon from pneumonia in April, 1923. The Countess of Carnarvon continued the arrangements with the Egyptian Government, but with some changes. Things however, continued to get worse, until at crisis point, the Egyptian Government denied Carter access to the tomb to continue his work. It was not until January 25th, 1925, that he was able to continue excavating. After careful diplomacy, agreements had been reached and a new concession signed. The work started with good will on both sides, all costs being borne by the Egyptian Government.

During Carter's absence his faithful workmen had kept an eye on the tomb, as they had done in 1923, when one wrote the following letter to Howard Carter in England.

Honourable Sir,

Beg to write this letter hoping that you are enjoying good health, and asking the Almighty to keep you and bring you back to us in Safety.

Beg to inform your Excellency that Store No. 15 is alright, Treasure is Alright, the Northern Store is alright. Wadain and House are alright and in all your work order is carried on according to your honourable instructions.

Rais Hussein, Gad Hassan, Hussein Awad, Abdelal Ahmed and all the Gaffirs of the house beg to send their regards.

My best regards to your respectable Self, and all members of the Lord's family, and to all your friends in England.

Longing to your early coming.

Your Most Obedient Servant

Ruis Ahmed Gurgar.

CHAPTER SEVEN

MUMMY

The third season's work was short as it started at the peak of the tourist season. Everyone wanted to see Tutankhamun's tomb and The Valley was crowded with visitors. Work within the tomb was therefore very difficult and the time was spent preparing objects that had been removed from the burial chamber the previous season, for transport to the Cairo Museum, where they were immediately put on display.

Work on the coffins of the King did not start in earnest until the fourth season, which began later that year. Howard Carter left London on September 23rd, 1925, and arrived in Cairo on the 28th, where as usual, he had to attend to formalities. Monsieur Lacau was not in Cairo at the time but on holiday in Europe. As Carter was sure that he would want to be present during the examination of the King's mummy, he cabled Lacau asking if he intended to be present. The reply came the following morning in the affirmative, asking for things to be delayed until he arrived. The date for the examination was then fixed for the 11th November.

Work on the tomb began once again with the removal of the filling, which had been replaced, as it was the best way of securing the tomb from unwanted visitors as well as protecting it from the elements. The day was

October 10th, over a month before the appointed time for the examination. Carter thought he had ample time to prepare everything, but as it was, he finished only just in time. The removal of the coffins was not to be as easy as he had thought.

To reach the King's mummy the encasing coffins had to be removed and when the operation started Carter had no idea how many there would be. The first great coffin entirely filled the quartzite sarcophagus. The lid was attached to the shell by means of 10 silver tongues which fitted into sockets, and secured by gold headed silver pins. Scaffolding had been erected round and over the sarcophagus. With the aid of self braking pulleys the lid was lifted off by its original silver handles, which were still strong enough to support its weight.

There was an air of expectancy in the tomb as the great lid rose from its base. What would they see within? Would it be as marvellous as what they had seen up till now, or would they be disappointed? At first they were not certain, for the inner coffin was covered with a thin shroud of linen, dark and much decayed. Scattered on top were floral wreaths and garlands. They had to wait several days before they were to see what lay beneath the shroud, for it had to be photographed, and Harry Burton the photographer, had not yet arrived.

On October 17, two days after his arrival, Burton photographed the coffin and work proceeded. The great depth of the sarcophagus and the fact that neither of the two coffins discovered so far could stand much handling in their existing positions, prompted Carter to remove them from the sarcophagus. This was achieved as before, using pulleys and by attaching steel pins to the tongue sockets of the outer coffin. The weight of the combined coffins was immense, far greater than they had anticipated. The pulleys held, however, and with great difficulty the coffins were raised above the sarcophagus so that wooden planks could be inserted beneath them. Carter now had to be something of an acrobat, balancing on these planks, bent low over the coffins, with the ceiling of the tomb just a few inches above his head.

Undeterred, he began to roll back the wrappings covering the second coffin. It was the finest example of an Egyptian coffin Carter had ever seen, showing the King in the form of the mummified god Osiris. Extremely beautiful and elegant, it was 6 feet 8 inches long, carved in wood covered in sheet gold and inlaid with coloured glass cut and engraved to simulate lapis lazuli, red jasper and turquoise. This was indeed a masterpiece of Egyptian art.

Having seen what was before them, a major problem became evident. How on earth were they going to be able to remove this coffin from the outer one? There were no handles, and it fitted so tightly into the outer coffin that it would prove impossible to pass straps underneath it. It was really a problem, for it was a full two days before a plan was devised to cope with it. Like the outer coffin, Carter had noticed that this one too had its lid fastened by means of silver pins. These were tightly secured, and as the coffin then was, could not be moved more than a quarter of an inch. Carter's plan was to secure stout copper wire around the pins, so that the coffin could be attached to the lifting tackle. Metal eyelets were also attached to the rim of the shell of the outer coffin, and then attached to a pulley on the scaffolding over the sarcophagus. The idea was to hold the inner coffin in position and slowly lower the outer coffin back into the sarcophagus. It was a daring plan and Carter knew it, but there were no alternatives, so with his heart almost in his mouth he began the operation. Slowly but surely the outer coffin fell away from the inner coffin, which was left for a brief moment suspended in mid air. Then swiftly, a wooden plank was inserted across the top of the sarcophagus, and the coffin was laid to rest. Although the worst was over, Carter's heart was still racing. His nerves were on edge. He knew how delicate the operation was and it was not finished yet. Although the coffin appeared quite strong, it could fall apart at any moment. The surface was already a little weak and could be damaged easily, and he had no idea of the condition of the wood beneath the gold. He had been lucky up till now, but he still had to remove the lid.

As there were no handles to the lid, he decided to screw in metal eyelets at places where no permanent damage could be done. To these he attached the lifting tackle. After removing the silver pins, which by this time were accessible, he began raising the lid. At first it appeared to stick, but it gradually came away and was gently lowered beside the coffin.

Excitedly they all peered inside. Like its predecessor, its contents were wrapped in a linen shroud. An elaborate floral and bead collarette lay on the neck and breast of the mummified form. Photography over, they removed the collarette and shroud which crumbled at their touch, and received a shock. By now Carter thought that nothing would surprise him, having been conditioned by all the wonderful sights that he had seen over the past years, but what he saw before him was too wonderful for words.

The third coffin was of solid gold ! Tutankhamun was truly the Golden Monarch, surely no other king in history was so honoured in death.

The mystery of the fantastic weight of the coffins was solved. All six feet one and three quarter inches of this third coffin was made of solid gold. This magnificent coffin is perhaps the foremost masterpiece of Egyptian art, certainly the most spectacular discovery in the tomb

E

itself. Its shape was like that of the other coffins, showing the King as the mummified god Osiris, but the features of the King were more youthful. The body was engraved with feathers and the figures Isis and Nephthys. Also superimposed in cloisonné on the engraved ornament of the coffin were the protective figures of Nekhebet and Buto, emblems of Upper and Lower Egypt, over which the young King had ruled. The inlay was of semi-precious stones. In addition to the collarette in cloisonné on the coffin, there was a detachable necklace of red and yellow gold, and blue faience.

The beauty of the work could not be wholly appreciated as it was disfigured by a black mass, the remains of the funerary oils that had been poured over the coffin. These oils had consolidated and stuck the gold coffin to the shell of the second coffin. Buckets of unguents must have been poured over the casket. Here lay the cause of much of the decomposition that had taken place within the sarcophagus.

The gold coffin, in the shell of the second coffin, was now moved with the aid of the muscle power of eight men into the antechamber, where it could be examined under better conditions. Once in the chamber the full magnitude of their discovery dawned upon them. There in their midst was the coffin of the King, more than six feet in length and about three and a half millimetres thick. A king's ransom in gold !

The outer casing of the second coffin was now treated with paraffin wax, to prevent it disintegrating while being handled. They then directed their attention to the black substance, which filled the gap between the two coffins and which covered much of the surface of the gold one. The chemist, Mr. Lucas, made a preliminary analysis of the substance, which appeared to soften with heat but was not affected by solvents.

Carter decided that before doing anything drastic he

would remove the lid. The line between the case and lid was clear and accessible. As in the case of the other coffins it was held in position by nails, in this case driven through eight gold tenons that held the lid in place. It was not possible to remove the nails as before, so they were sacrificed and the heads cut through.

Now at last, as Carter had anticipated, he came face to face with the King. For there, inside the gold coffin lay the mummy of the King, adorned with a magnificent gold mask. The mask was a perfect portrait of Tutankhamun as he must have looked shortly before his death. The workmanship was beyond description. It has since become almost the symbol of Tutankhamun, instantly recognisable by most people with only the slightest interest in the past.

The mummy was beautifully arranged and bound with bands of gold enclosing gold trappings and other funerary paraphernalia. Burnished gold hands which had originally held the crook and flail were sewn on to the linen wrappings. The crook and flail had disintegrated, owing to the fact that like the outside of the coffin, the inside too had been drenched with funerary oil. The oil had hardened into a black mass and although not poured on the gold mask itself, it had seeped underneath and around the sides, fixing it to the gold coffin.

The gold bands were inscribed. One down the centre recorded a welcoming speech of Nut, the Goddess of the Sky. It read

"I reckon thy beauties, O Osiris, King Kheperu-neb-Re (Tutankhamun) thy soul livest; thy veins are firm. Thou smellest the air and goest out as a god, going out as Atum, O Osiris Tutankhamun. Thou goest out and thou enterest with Ra ..."

When all these trappings were removed several interesting facts were discovered. The first was that originally they were not made the correct size. The mummy must have been larger than anticipated, and some parts of the trappings had to be added to, while others had to be cut. Another fascinating fact that emerged was that several pieces appeared to be surplus from the burial of Smenkhkare. On the back of some cloisonné plaques were texts from the 'Chapter of the Heart', where in places the names of Smenkhkare were inscribed, though in most cases they were defaced.

Although Carter tried a number of methods to separate the coffins in time for the examination of the mummy, all were unsuccessful and on the day appointed the examination had to be carried out with the mummy still resting in the coffins.

Tests had shown that the only way that they were going to be able to separate the coffins was with heat. They had already tried sun heat which had reached a temperature of 149° F. (65° C.), but nothing had happened, now their only hope was to use external heat, in this case several Primus paraffin lamps.

By this time the mummy had been removed but the gold mask was still stuck fast by the black mass. Carter knew that he had to take great care, one false move, and treasure that had survived centuries would be lost in a moment forever. The coffins were turned upside down on trestles, the interior of the gold coffin having previously been lined with a thick layer of zinc plates. The outside of the coffins were covered with blankets saturated in water, to keep the coffins cool. The idea was to place the paraffin burners under the gold coffin. The zinc plates would provide a suitable safeguard for the underneath, ensuring that the heat did not rise above the melting point of zinc, which is low, while the paraffin wax on the surface of the second coffin would act as a good indicator if things got too hot on the outside.

After about two hours at a temperature in the region

of 500° C., things began to happen. The lamps were turned out. After a while the second coffin was lifted off, leaving the gold coffin inverted on the trestles. It was covered with a dripping mass of black goo, which proved extremely difficult to remove even with the help of solvents. During the operation the gold mask had been protected by a wet blanket, which was kept saturated with water. The heat also did the trick here, and the mask was removed with little difficulty.

After the second coffin had been removed, the outer coffin was again lifted from the sarcophagus and sent off to the laboratory. This left only the bier to be lifted out, which fortunately was accomplished with ease. Thus ended probably the most exciting part of the whole saga of the discovery of the tomb.

CHAPTER EIGHT

★

TUTANKHAMUN

Of all we know about the Ancient Egyptian way of life and death, perhaps the greatest interest has been in the process of mummification, which has helped to give Egyptology its mysterious appeal. Luckily the mummy of Tutankhamun, was to everyone's surprise intact, although not in as good a condition as was hoped. There are few royal mummies that survive today, which have not at some time or other been rifled by robbers, who in their frantic search for jewels and gold, have torn the wrappings and left the corpse damaged and exposed to the atmosphere.

Mummification of the body was to the Egyptians an important part of religion and their belief in life after death. Early in Egyptian Prehistory, the body was preserved quite naturally by burial in hot dry sand, which acted as an efficient dehydrating agent. A good example of a body preserved in this way is "Ginger", whose Pre-Dynastic burial is reconstructed beneath glass in the British Museum, although recently some aspersions have been cast about his authenticity. It appears that during the 19th century, the British Museum badly needed a Pre-Dynastic burial and this need was dutifully filled by a rather notorious antiquities dealer, whose brother had disappeared in mysterious circumstances ! The British Museum, however, are quite satisfied and are not willing to put "Ginger" to the test and sacrifice what may be a perfectly genuine exhibit.

When burial became more sophisticated, entailing the use of a sort of chamber, this natural dehydration process could not take place. Several attempts were made to overcome this, in one of them the body was tightly wrapped in bandages to protect it from the air. This was a dismal failure, the result was even more rapid decomposition. Experiments continued. Egyptologists are fairly sure that by the Fourth Dynasty, (c. 2613-2494 B.C.) the Egyptian embalmers had realized that the most necessary step towards preservation was the removal of the internal organs. Bandaged packets of viscera soaking in a dilute solution of natron, a naturally occurring compound of sodium carbonate and sodium bicarbonate, have been found in a tomb of this period. During the Old and Middle Kingdom, (c. 2686-1786 B.C.) no fixed method of preparing the corpse was practised, in some cases the viscera were removed, in others the brain. Sometimes the body had been dehydrated, and few well preserved bodies remain today. By the New Kingdom, (c. 1567-1085 B.C.) the embalmers understood the basic requirements of preservation, although the results weren't always as good as they might have been. It took seventy days between death and interment, to prepare the corpse for burial. Half of this time had to be devoted to the drying process. The embalmers' first task was to remove the parts which would decay first, the internal organs, by making an incision in the left side of the chest, and the brain, by making a hole inside the nose. It used to be thought that the body was then soaked for a long period in a bath of natron, although recent studies have shown it more probable that natron was used dry. This had the effect of efficiently dehydrating the body, dissolving body fats and leaving the skin supple. The viscera were treated with natron separately. All the materials used in this process would be preserved and buried either in the tomb or near to it, as it was thought that the essential body juices extracted in the embalming process must not be completely divorced from the mummy.

The body would then be padded, any incisions sewn up, and covered with a plate of leather or other material decorated with an "Eye of Horus", a powerful protective talisman. The eye sockets were plugged with linen or set with artificial eyes. The body was then treated with resins, ointment and spices, and covered with a series of bandages between which were placed protective charms, the most important being the heart scarab, which was placed on the breast. It was during this last process of bandaging that the Egyptian embalmers did their utmost to restore the original shape of the body. The internal organs would then be placed in four special containers called Canopic jars, with stoppers in the form of various heads, a jackal, an ape, a falcon and a human, into which would be placed the stomach, intestines, lungs and liver. At a later period, when the viscera were packed separately and replaced inside the body, dummy Canopic jars were used in order to carry on the tradition of centuries.

The term "mummy" comes from the Arabic word meaning "a body preserved in bitumen", "mumiya" being the Arabic word for bitumen. This has led to the popular misconception that a corpse was mummified by treatment with the substance. As we now know bitumen was not normally used in the process at all. A number of written accounts exist describing mummification. The Greek writer Herodotus describes the process in detail, but his information is sometimes inaccurate, and is based on the mummification techniques of about the 5th century B.C.

It was not until November 11th 1925 that the mummy

of Tutankhamun could be examined. Now at last, perhaps they would find out more about this mysterious monarch, who had left so many wonderful treasures and yet so little information about himself. How old was he really ? How did he die ? What did he look like ? There were many important questions which remained to be answered. Perhaps the examination would also provide a clue to his real identity. The autopsy created a rather macabre scene in the tomb. The group, included Egyptian Government officials and dignitaries; Pierre Lacau, Director-General of the Department of Antiquities; Mr. A. Lucas, chemist of the Department of Antiquities; Mr. Harry Burton of the Metropolitan Museum of Art; the Chief Inspector of Antiquities; Howard Carter; and Dr. Saleh Bey Hamdi. All watched fascinated as Dr. Derry, Professor of Anatomy of the Egyptian University, who was conducting the examination, made his first moves. The first snags soon became apparent.

He found it extremely difficult to conduct a proper examination, as the mummy of the King and the magnificent gold death mask which covered his head, shoulders and part of his chest were firmly stuck by a pitch-like substance, to the bottom of the coffin in which they had rested for so long. This was due to unguents which had been poured over the mummy after it had been placed in the coffin, which with the passing of time had dried to a stony hardness. The linen bandages were in an extremely fragile condition and crumbled at the slightest touch. It appeared that the humidity of the air at the time of entombment and the decomposition of the oils that had been poured over the body, had created a high temperature which had deteriorated the bandages.

Rather than let the wrappings crumble before their eyes, Carter suggested that they should be strengthened with warm wax. This having been done, the only course open to them was to cut the bandages, as it was unfortunately impossible to unwrap the mummy layer by layer as they had hoped. The first incision was only a few millimetres deep but it enabled the bandages to be turned outwards, revealing a number of talismans. As the examination continued, it became increasingly obvious that the wrappings were in an advanced state of decay and were in some cases reduced to dust.

Enclosed in the many layers of wrappings were a vast number of personal and mystical ornaments. Every layer that was removed revealed more and more. These objects were mostly amulets, religious devices intended to protect the mummy from evil spirits, and to guide the soul through the dangers it was to meet in the Nether World. Egyptologists are not sure about the powers or names of many of these charms, except that they were for the protection and guidance of the dead and were to be as fine and expensive as possible. For the mummy of Tutankhamun they were the finest. From the neck to the abdomen were thirty-five objects in seventeen groups, between thirteen layers of bandaging, including a very large pectoral collar in chased sheet gold which extended over the shoulders of the King. Other objects included numerous amulets, pendants and collars and other items of personal jewellery.

The King lay with his arms across his body. Each arm, from the elbow to the wrist, was covered with bracelets of gold, silver and semi-precious stones, six on the left and seven on the right. All his limbs were bandaged separately and then included in the overall bandaging. His fingers and toes were wrapped individually and then covered with gold sheaths, and in the case of the feet, gold sandals were bandaged in position. It was not until the greater part of the bandages had been removed, and the pitch-like mass that held the mummy forcibly chiselled away, that Tutankhamun's remains could be released and lifted from the coffin. Close examination could then take place.

The bandages that covered the head of the King seemed to be in a better state of preservation than the rest of the body, perhaps the only exception being the feet, a situation possibly explained by the fact that these areas had not been saturated with unguents, as had the rest of the mummy. At the top of the head they found a pad in the shape of a crown, made from wads of linen, which had probably served the purpose of filling the empty space between the skull and the gold mask.

Beneath this pad was a small amuletic pillow or head-rest of iron, a rare metal during the 18th Dynasty, and found only three times on the mummy. After they had removed a few more layers of wrapping, they came across a magnificent gold diadem which completely encircled the King's head. The diadem was a ribbon-like band of gold and cornelian, which ended at the back of the head with a floral and disc-shaped bow. This extremely beautiful example of the goldsmiths' art bore the insignia of sovereignty of northern and southern Egypt. It was adjustable at the back, for in life it would have been worn over a wig or crown or both.

Underneath the next layers of linen, around the forehead was a broad burnished gold temple-band, terminating behind and above the ears, where there were slots through which linen tapes were passed and tied in a bow at the back of the head. This band held in place a fine linen head-dress, unfortunately in an advanced state of decay and hardly recognisable except for a kind of pigtail at the back. Beneath this and more layers of bandaging was a linen skull cap, which fitted tightly over the shaven head of the King, and was held in place by another gold band. Embroidered with an elaborate design in minute gold and faience beads, it too was badly decayed, although the beadwork had survived almost intact. They decided not to remove this cap as it would serve little purpose, and so they covered it with a thin coat of wax and left it in position.

The removal of the final bandage from the King's face was an extremely delicate operation, as the head was in such a bad state of preservation. The danger of damaging the delicate features as the wrappings came away, was uppermost in their minds. Dr. Derry then removed the final fragments of wrapping with a fine brush. The face of the monarch, who had ended his reign over three thousand years earlier, was then revealed before them. A serene, refined and cultured face, his features were well formed and lips clearly marked. Plugs filled his nostrils. His eyes were partly open and had in no way been interfered with, except to be covered with fabric impregnated with resin. His skin was a greyish colour, very brittle and cracked, yet it was difficult to realize that this was the face of a man, who lived 3,324 years ago, and which had survived intact to face the world of the twentieth century. His eyelashes were very long. The soft upper part of the nose had been flattened by the pressure of the bandages, and as the upper lip was slightly turned upwards, the front incisor teeth could be seen. His ears were small and well formed and had holes approximately 7·5 mm. in diameter punctured in the lobes. Dr. Derry noticed two abrasions in the skin of the forehead, which may have been caused by pressure of the bandages against the diadem the King was wearing. A rounded depression on the left side of the cheek, in front of the ear lobe with slightly discoloured skin surrounding it, was taken by Dr. Derry to be a scab, although he could not suggest what had caused it.

The most striking thing about the features of the mummy to those who watched it being unwrapped, was how amazingly accurate the contemporary artists had been. The goldsmith who fashioned the magnificent death mask left for posterity, in imperishable gold, a highly accurate record of the King as he was in life. Indeed, with the evidence of the mummy before them, it was clear that all the artists who portrayed Tutankhamun did so with amazing perception. Their works in wood, stone, gold, plaster and precious stones show a young, gentle, fine featured, good looking man, as he clearly was.

As for the skull itself, Dr. Derry found it to be a very uncommon type, broad and flat topped (platycephalic) measuring a quite remarkable 155·5 mm. across. It was empty, except for some resinous material that the embalmers had introduced through the nose, after extracting the brain. The King's wisdom teeth seemed to have erupted only a short time before his death.

As already mentioned the body was in an extremely brittle state. Examination of the abdomen revealed the embalming incision on the left side, 86 mm. in length. The right side had a marked bulge, due to the stuffing of the abdominal cavity from the incision on the left. The whole of the abdominal cavity was filled with a mass of rock-hard resin and linen. An unusual feature was that the talismanic plate, which usually covers the abdominal incision on mummies, was absent. However, an oval gold plate was found on the left side in the vicinity of the wound, while the mummy was being stripped of its wrappings.

Dr. Derry's examination of the sexual organs revealed no signs of pubic hair and he found it impossible to say whether the King had been circumcised. The phallus was wrapped independently after having been drawn forward. It was then incorporated in the erect position with the rest of the abdomen by the perinial bandages.

It was now clear from the remains that the portraits made of the King were extremely accurate, but the principal reason for examining his body was to determine his age at death, and if possible, the cause of death. To determine the former, Dr. Derry decided to examine the epiphysis (the growing end of long bones) of the tibia (shin bone) and femur (thigh bone). The epiphysis is that part of the bone which ossifies (turns into bone) separately, eventually becoming part of the main bone. During childhood and adolescence the epiphyses are attached to the main bone by cartilage. The times of ossification are known, therefore examination of the joints of the King should provide a clue to his age. Examination of the femur showed that the lower end was still not united. This part is known to ossify at about the age of twenty, therefore he was younger than this. The trochanter at the upper end of the thigh bone was entirely fused to the main bone, but a definite gap still existed on its inner side, showing that the union was still incomplete. This part is known to ossify at about the age of eighteen in males. The epiphysis of the head of the femur also ossifies at about the same age, and this too was found to be fused, but the line of the marriage could still be seen clearly. The upper end of the tibia was still not united, while the lower portion was fused, a condition known to occur at about the age of eighteen. On this evidence Dr. Derry concluded that Tutankhamun would have been eighteen or over, but under twenty when he died. Examination of the upper arm bones confirmed his conclusions. To act as a control he used X-rays of young Egyptians, as he was of the opinion that the epiphyses united earlier in Egyptians than in Europeans. He concluded there was little room for doubt on the approximate age of the King, but suggested that it may be possible to add or subtract a year.

Unfortunately, Dr. Derry found it impossible to ascertain the cause of death. The King had died young, but there was no clue as to whether or not he had met his death naturally. Evidence of poison would probably have been destroyed by the mummification process, and there were no visible signs on the body of a wound other than the embalming incision.

Although unable to supply the cause of death, Dr. Derry was able to give a reasonable description of how the King would have looked when alive. He was slightly built, and would have stood approximately 5 ft. 6 in. high. The skeleton actually measured 5 ft. 4½ in., but there would have been some shrinkage. It was obvious from the head that the portraits were life like. Measurements of the two life-size black figures of the King that had stood in the antechamber, showed that the sculptures were very accurate indeed and probably gave a very good impression of how the King looked in life. Perhaps the best portrait of all, though, was the golden mask. Before the examination was finished, measurements were taken of all the dimensions of the skull and skeleton.

CHAPTER NINE

★

INCEST

Thus the discoverers and the learned doctors came face to face with Tutankhamun. They had examined the vast treasure of the King and had now examined the King himself. They felt extremely close, yet separated in time by over three millennia. A great deal was known about the King through his possessions and through the tell-tale clues found on the mummy itself, but although they had been able to answer some questions, they did not know at that time the whole truth about Tutankhamun. Today, nearly fifty years after the discovery, with the vast amount of research, other excavations in the interval, and the results of investigations carried out by using modern scientific techniques, we can begin to fit together the pieces of this gigantic jigsaw to reveal a story entangled in a web of royal incest and political and religious intrigue. It is extremely difficult to sift through all the clues and red herrings to piece together all the evidence, but it can be done.

In this saga the reign of Tutankhamun occupies the penultimate chapter. He is almost in the position of being in the final act of a dramatic thriller, but like any good thriller, it is quite useless to read the final chapter divorced from the beginning.

Tutankhamun, it is thought, was born around 1361

B.C., towards the end of the Egyptian 18th Dynasty. During the 18th Dynasty, which was about 1567-1320 B.C., Egypt held a prominent position in the civilized world of the Eastern Mediterranean, due to her wealth, power and resources. For agriculture Egypt was like an oasis in the middle of the desert of North Africa, as her crops were not at the mercy of the weather for a good or bad season. The Nile, which was the life source of this great empire, annually watered and fertilised the fields, its suspension of red silt giving at least one crop a season. Under the strong control of a centralised government, a portion of each year's harvest was stored for the next year's seed and also for times of need. The vast majority of the population were farmers whose work was continuous and largely concerned with irrigation, such as building dams, piercing dykes and watering the higher lying fields. It was to this virtual paradise that many wandering herders descended in their annual migration to richer pastures.

Egypt had a large population of domestic animals, such as oxen, sheep, pigs, donkeys, goats and also at this time horses. She also had great natural resources. The papyrus reed which grew wild in profusion was perhaps one of the most important, as it could be used for many things from food to building materials, and provided the vital paper for the Egyptian Civil Service and for written records of all kinds. Her lands were rich with aromatic woods and resins, and her deserts famous for their rich deposits of gold, salt, natron — a naturally occurring compound of sodium carbonate and sodium bicarbonate, minerals, and precious and semi-precious stones. She was also a great centre of trade, supplying the commodities of tropical Africa to the lands of the Mediterranean, either in their raw state or manufactured into consumer goods by the almost unequalled skill of the Egyptian craftsmen.

F

The basic social unit of all classes was the family. In the agricultural community several families would form a village settlement under a mayor or headman. Many farmers were landowners, former mercenaries who had been given land as a reward for their services, although a large proportion of the farmers were tenants of the important land owners, the temples of Memphis, Heliopolis and Thebes and also the Treasury and Royal Harems. All paid taxes in grain to the State granaries. At times when the fields were under water and the peasantry largely unemployed, the State put this large potential work-force to good use for public works such as brick-making, clearing, and the construction of buildings.

Although the Pharaoh was the supreme ruler, the day-to-day business was carried out by the administrative class, who unlike the masses, could read and write, and who acted either as the servants of the Pharaoh, or of the officials to whom he had delegated some of his power. There is no doubt that this literate administrative class was responsible for the organisation which made Egypt a great empire, for when it began to break down, so did Egypt. Work was organised on an hereditary basis with the eldest son taking over the job of his father within the literate classes, the younger sons automatically becoming scribes if their father's job was not open to them. The only exception to this time honoured rule that applied to all, was introduced during the New Kingdom (about 1567-1085 B.C.) when the army provided an opportunity for great promotion by faithful service, even from the lower classes. By the 18th Dynasty a new class had grown up, the professional fighters who took the place of conscripted peasants. Such a class had evolved with the introduction of the horse-drawn chariot and had spread all over the Near East, bringing a new emphasis on athletic ability and the skills of war. This is particularly noticeable in portrayals of the Pharaoh himself, whose role changes from the divine yet impassive figure-head, to the superhumanly athletic warrior at the head of his army, often in his chariot, slaying the enemies of his empire. Regardless of age or actual physical ability, the Pharaoh is shown as a hero whether with his army or shooting lions.

With this new military prowess the Pharaoh re-established the old authority of the Crown which had suffered during the preceding period, due to the rise of feudalism when his power had been diminished and claimed by local governors. Such all-powerful leadership brought victories, extending over Asia, Nubia and the Sudan, wealth, and unparalleled economic expansion that rose to a peak during the reign of Amenophis III and then declined. The Pharaoh owned the whole land with everything in it, men, animals, resources; they all belonged to him, he was god incarnate.

It was the 18th Dynasty, the Dynasty in which Tutankhamun was to reign, which produced some of the most victorious warring Pharaohs in Egyptian history. At the beginning of the Dynasty, the Pharaoh Amosis, largely established the policy of his successors. As ruler of a then united Upper and Lower Egypt he took immediate steps to secure his fortresses in the north, and the east and west Delta, re-establish Egyptian control of Nubia, centralise the country's administration and re-open the trade routes to Africa, Asia, and the Greek islands. He also continued the pressure against Egypt's old enemy the Hyksos, the Semitic immigrants who had threatened her territories for centuries, as far as southern Palestine. He recovered land as far south as the Second Cataract of the Nile, although hindered by subversive activity in Nubia. Amosis also cleverly created a new office of Viceroy of Kush, who was to be a high ranking and trusted official whose job would be to promote Egyptian policy in Nubia, a very important position that was to be maintained throughout the New Kingdom. This new policy of aggression was continued by Amosis' immediate successors, Amenophis I and Tuthmosis I, who extended the southern boundary well beyond the Third Cataract and re-established fortresses built during the Middle Kingdom, campaigning vigorously against the Libyans in the west. With this re-affirmed, strong and united country, came a new revival in temple building, especially at Karnak, as gratitude to the gods for victory, and also a renaissance in art which was to leave for all time the artists' view of the great conquering Pharaohs. Tuthmosis I in particular, who reigned about 1525-1512 B.C., drove his armies as far as the Euphrates, defeating the great kingdom of Mitanni and left a stone monument or stela on the eastern bank to commemorate his victory. It was Tuthmosis I who was the first to build his tomb in the remote Valley of the Kings, and so set the pattern for all the Pharaohs of the New Kingdom.

Unfortunately Tuthmosis II who succeeded Tuthmosis I was to be an exception to his predecessors, as he suffered from poor health and was unable to carry out such aggressive campaigns.

He died young, leaving his heir, Tuthmosis III who was just a boy to succeed him. Because of the age of the new king, his stepmother Queen Hatshepsut acted as his regent for a few years, until she completely took control and had herself declared ruler. She reigned for about twenty years, of which little is known for certain, except perhaps, that during this time the country's resources were devoted to the peaceful activities of the arts.

Tuthmosis III finally managed to regain the throne in about 1482 B.C., either by force or the death of his stepmother we don't know. His new regime was openly hostile to the memory of Hatshepsut and did all in its power to mutilate and destroy anything that testified to her existence. At this time a revolt of the subject princes in Syria resulted in the withdrawal of Egyptian garrisons to southern Palestine. Tuthmosis III reacted with great vigour and in 1481 B.C. defeated the rebel princes at Megiddo. Not content with re-establishing Egyptian control in western Asia, he gained control eastward across the Euphrates, northward to the boundaries of the Hittite Empire, and southward beyond the Fourth Cataract in the Sudan, in a series of brilliantly executed campaigns. This newly acquired territory was then held by trusted local princes whose loyalty was stimulated by Egyptian viceroys. In Egypt itself, new temples were built and the arts flourished, the craftsmen making use of the wealth of precious materials now available.

His successor Amenophis II, who we know was exceptionally tall and strong for an Egyptian king, took his armies further south in the Sudan than any Pharaoh before him. The next Pharaoh, Tuthmosis IV, continued in the same tradition, strengthening prestige in Asia and consolidating his position by marrying the daughter of the King of Mitanni, the powerful state lying between the empires of Egypt and the Hittites.

By the time the son of Tuthmosis IV, Amenophis III, came to the throne, Egypt had reached its zenith with the empire abroad secure and unparalleled prosperity at home. So secure was the empire that Amenophis III, unlike his predecessors, had only to make a punative exepedition to the Sudan and a few tours of western Asia in the early years of his reign. He was one of the longest reigning Pharaohs of the Dynasty and ruled for nearly forty years. It was a time of opulence and luxury. With Egypt a mighty empire at the hub of the civilized world, she was exposed to the culture, taste and riches of a cosmopolitan society. The traditional and stiff Egyptian art forms that had been accepted throughout the Dynasty, mellowed under the influence of a Court and society thronging with foreign princesses and their entourages and became more vital, realistic and exacting. Craftsmen, sculptors, architects and painters, were encouraged to equal the great artistic demands placed upon them, and the result was some of the finest achievements of Egyptian art.

Luckily for us today, Amenophis III, throughout his time on the throne, had a large number of commemorative scarabs made to celebrate the important events of his reign, in a similar way that medals are struck in modern times. These invaluable written accounts were issued to record such things as the King's hunting skills, ceremonies at which he officiated, to commemorate his three jubilees, or whenever he strengthened his country's relations with foreign kings by marrying their daughters. We learn from one of these scarabs that in Year 10, a foreign princess, Gilukhepa, daughter of King Shuttarna of Mitanni, was received into his harem. Year 10 in this case would mean the tenth year of the reign of Amenophis III, as Egyptian dates started and ended with the reign of the Pharaoh, and began again from Year I of his successor. During such a long and peaceful reign, Amenophis III was able to devote himself to extensive building operations and to the patronage of the arts. Important buildings were erected in most of the larger centres and many great temples constructed, including the temple of Luxor, which was of a most unusual design, dedicated to the god of the empire, Amen-Re. In the Sudan a number of temples were built, in some of which the King himself was worshipped as a god, a clever form of royal propaganda.

Our story really starts with the son of Amenophis III, Amenophis IV, later known as Akhenaten, the heretic king. To avoid confusion we shall refer to him as Akhenaten throughout.

It was not unusual in Ancient Egypt for a Pharaoh to

take his brother, his half brother or his son as co-regent, especially if he had already ruled for a long period and was getting old. Amenophis III celebrated a number of jubilees in his long reign and it is quite possible that he appointed his son as co-regent. Whether he did or not is most important to our story, for our time-table of events must be based on it. Egyptologists do not agree on this issue. There are some who do not believe in a co-regency at all, others who do, but believe the period to be short. The concensus of opinion today is, however, that there was a co-regency between Amenophis III and Akhenaten his son, which lasted a number of years. Cyril Aldred, the well known Egyptologist, has made a convincing case for the co-regency and has presented reliable evidence to support it. For our purposes, it need only be said that co-regency was practised during the 18th Dynasty, an obvious example being the well recorded yet short period of joint rule between Akhenaten and Smenkhkare. Co-regency had a number of advantages, one being that it established the elder king as supreme ruler without threat from his successor. It ensured the succession of the Dynasty and also allowed the new king to serve a period akin to apprenticeship.

In order to establish the identity of Tutankhamun, it is necessary at this stage to try to establish the relationships between members of the royal family, his immediate predecessors. Amenophis III was directly descended from the long line of 18th Dynasty Pharaohs, his father being Tuthmosis IV and his mother Mutemwiya, a Mitannian princess. Amenophis III married Tiye and made her his Chief Wife and Queen.

The story that now begins to unfold is fascinating in the extreme, though a little complicated, for at most all we have to fit the clues together is circumstantial evidence. It is rather like assembling a gigantic jigsaw puzzle whose parts fit each other and which can be assembled in a number of ways to make several different pictures. The picture we are about to see is the most understandable and attractive.

The complication seems to have started in the reign of Tuthmosis IV, who reigned for only a short period of about nine years. It was the practice in the 18th Dynasty to pass on succession to the throne through a royal daughter. The male heir did not automatically become Pharaoh, his right of succession had to be confirmed by marriage to a royal princess, probably his sister or half sister. This had been the practice throughout the 18th Dynasty, but was to be interrupted at this point. It is more than probable that Tuthmosis IV died without a surviving heiress with whom his son could marry, thereby confirming his right to the throne. This may have been due to the high infant mortality rate of the time, for we know that Tuthmosis IV had at least one son and a daughter, who were interred with him in his tomb in the Biban-el-Moluk at Thebes, and who had died before their father. Thus it was necessary for his son, Amenophis III, to marry outside the dynastic family.

Amenophis III chose Tiye, the daughter of Tuyu, and Yuya, a powerful nobleman who held an influential position at Court, being Master of the Horse and Lieutenant of the King's Chariots. Both he and his wife seem to have come from Akhmim, in Nubia, the capital of the ninth province of Upper Egypt. The family had extensive estates there and Yuya was Prophet and Superintendent of Cattle to the god Min. Tuyu was Superior of the Harem of Min, and at Thebes she held the important position of Superior of the Harem of Amun. The mummies of Tuyu and Yuya were found in 1903 in a small tomb in the eastern valley of the Biban-el-Moluk. As usual, the tomb had been rifled and its contents badly disturbed, but most of the funerary equipment was still there. The coffins had been disturbed and both Tuyu and Yuya were exposed to the atmosphere. In spite of this, their mummies were exceptionally well preserved and we can imagine without much difficulty what they must have looked like in life. Yuya's head was long and he had white wavy hair. His nose was large and beaked and he had prominent lips. He was very tall and must have been a man of noble yet un-Egyptian appearance. Tuyu's features were very similar to the Egyptian peasant women of today.

Although Yuya, by his position in Court, and by the fact that he was a warrior of some standing, was of a status befitting that of father of the wife of a warrior king, there seems to have been another reason why Amenophis III should look towards his family for a wife. It is possible that Yuya was the son of a certain Yey, who may have been the father of Queen Mutemwiya, wife of Tuthmosis IV. Some scholars have suggested that Mutemwiya was the daughter of King Aratama of Mitanni, the nation that lay between the empires of Egypt and the Hittites. This seems very unlikely as although it was the practice of the Egyptian Pharaohs to marry the daughters of foreign kings, they occupied only a minor place at Court, and were merely absorbed into the Royal Harem. Queen Mutemwiya was an extremely important person and had great influence, an influence that was to continue during the first few years of the reign of her son, Amenophis III. In inscriptions she is simply described as an "heiress", unlike another member of the King's Harem, Queen Yaret, who is described as "King's sister" or "King's daughter."

There are two shawbati figures in the Metropolitan Museum of Art, New York, which have a bearing on our story and may help clarify relationships. They are inscribed for a "Father of the god and Master of the Horse, Yey." This inscription suggests that Yey had a daughter who married a Pharaoh. The figures appear to be middle 18th Dynasty, about the time of Tuthmosis IV. Now the name Yey is very similar to Yuya in Egyptian, and it is quite probable that Yey was Yuya's father, Yuya holding the same titles as "Father of the god and Master of the Horse." If such a surmise is correct, Yuya would have been the brother-in-law of Tuthmosis IV, and his daughter Tiye, would be the nearest in line of succession that Amenophis III could choose, as he had no sister. Therefore, although it appears that the break with dynastic tradition was a great one, it is purely circumstantial, and Amenophis III did his best to overcome it. It was, however, a further strengthening of a family who were to have almost overpowering influence throughout the reign of Amenophis III, Akhenaten, Smenkhkare, Tutankhamun, Ay, and even Horemheb.

In an effort to prevent his children being called bastards, Amenophis III went out of his way to publicise his marriage to the commoner Tiye. He had special commemorative scarabs issued on his wedding day, in Year 1 of his reign, in which he detailed for all to know the humble origins of his Queen. These were sent to all corners of the Empire. In the circumstances that have been outlined, marrying Tiye was the best that Amenophis III could do, but it not only broke a dynastic tradition, but also flaunted the religious doctrine, according to the rites of Amun. The divine right of succession was based on the idea that the god in the form of the monarch married the daughter of the god, a Pharaoh's daughter. The thought of the god consorting with a commoner was tantamount to heresy.

Although we have talked of Amenophis III "choosing" Tiye for his wife, and issuing commemorative scarabs to other rulers, announcing his marriage, it is unlikely that Amenophis carried out these acts unaided, for he could not have been more than nine years of age on his succession. What we are really seeing is the clever diplomacy of his mother Mutemwiya. In this way we first see the strong influence of Yuya's family beginning to mould the future of the 18th Dynasty.

Tiye seems to have been even younger than her husband, Amenophis III, for she outlived him, although he ruled for nearly forty years; she was still of child bearing age in about his thirty-ninth regnal year, when she bore him a daughter Beketaten. Another member of this powerful family, Tiye's brother, Anen, also held an influential position. He was second of the four prophets of Amun, and the Greatest of Seers in the temple of Re-Atum. He was also close to the King, Amenophis III, and doubtless officiated at many of the royal ceremonies. His loyalty was rewarded by the gift of a fine tomb at western Thebes. It is interesting that no mention is made of his relationship with the King in official documents or inscriptions, and we only know he was related to Tiye through an inscription on the coffin of Tuyu, their mother.

When we come to trace the children of Amenophis III and Tiye, it is not so easy. We know they had a son, born Amenophis IV, who changed his name to Akhenaten during his reign as Pharaoh. There was also a Prince Tuthmose, who may have been the heir-apparent as he held the position of High Priest of Ptah at Memphis, a role often filled by the heir-apparent. He must have died young as we hear little about him later, as it was Amenophis IV (Akhenaten) who succeeded to the throne. The name of Prince Tuthmose is inscribed on a few monuments in the Memphis area. The whip discovered in Tutankhamun's tomb, with the inscription, "The King's son and Captain of the Troops, Tuthmose" may well have been his. They also had a daughter, Sitamun, who became an important person in her own right. The youngest daughter Beketaten has already been mentioned. Sitamun is fairly well documented. Her portrait appears in the tomb of her grandparents, Tuyu and Yuya. She is shown seated in majesty receiving a golden necklace, while another scene shows her paying homage to her mother, Queen Tiye. She wears a tall wig and a crown of lotuses, a privilege usually given to princesses who had married their fathers. In inscriptions she is often referred to as "King's Chief Wife". It seems from overwhelming evidence, that there was an incestuous relationship between Amenophis III and his daughter, and that he married her and made her Queen. This marriage between father and daughter is unusual, even by Egyptian standards, for it was usual for brother to marry sister on ascending the throne, and therefore Sitamun should have married her brother, Akhenaten. Amenophis III may have taken this unusual step to strengthen his position on the throne, in that it could now be said that the god had married a daughter of the god. In this way began a series of subtle alterations in the line of descent and the royal geneology. Greater importance was attached to maternal descent and daughters became more important than sons. In none of the great monumental reliefs of this period are princes portrayed, and yet as we know, there were certainly male heirs. Sitamun lived at least to the 37th year of Amenophis III and probably outlived him.

Once again the male heir-apparent was not able to marry a royal daughter, for his father had married Sitamun, the only daughter yet born to Amenophis III and Tiye. Akhenaten therefore had to look elsewhere. We know from the numerous reliefs that he married Nefertiti, famous for her beauty. The wonderful portrait bust of her in the Berlin Museum is probably one of the best known pieces of Egyptian art. We marvel over her beauty today, but in her day too she was considered beautiful, her name meaning "a beautiful woman has come". Her un-Egyptian features have often been taken by some Egyptologists to suggest a foreign origin, but as we have suggested before, foreign princesses in Egypt were doomed to obscurity in the Royal Harems and never raised to the important status of Chief Wife. Marriages with foreign princesses were simply diplomatic. In order for us to identify the parents of Nefertiti, we must return our attention to the powerful family of Tuyu and Yuya.

We have already seen how their daughter, Tiye, became the Queen of Amenophis III, and how their son, Anen, held such an important position in the hierarchy at Thebes. Such a family with a tradition of warlike pursuits whose head held the position of Master of the Horse, would surely have had a son to continue the family tradition. It seems possible that Anen forsook this responsibility in preference for a religious career, so the family tradition may well have been continued by a younger son. Such a man appears at the Court of Akhenaten. He holds a position very close to the King, with most of the titles held by Yuya under Amenophis III. He too was Master of the Horse, he too was "one trusted by the good god (the King) in the entire land", he too was Foremost of the Companions of the King and "praised by the good god". These titles were honorific but it seems too much of a coincidence for these two men not to have been related in some way. His name was Ay, which is also very similar to Yuya in Egyptian and can be written Ay or Aya, as Yuya can be written Yey, a situation which suggests a close relationship between the two men. There is also other evidence, Ay built a rock-chapel at Akhmim to the local god Min, something an Egyptian would only normally do if it was his birth place or family seat, and if we remember that Yuya hailed from Akhmim where he had extensive estates, it seems more than likely that Ay was the son of Yuya. It was also the practice at the time for sons to be appointed to their father's job, which certainly seems to have been the case here. But there is one title we have not mentioned yet, which is very important and cannot be explained away as coincidence. Yuya was described as "Father of the god" a title used to denote he was father of the Queen. Ay too used the title "Father of the god", indicating that he also was father of the Queen. It seems very likely therefore, that he was the father of Nefertiti. Normally only maternal parentage was claimed, and if Ay was the father of Nefertiti we would expect her to call Ay's wife, Tey, "Mother of the King's Chief Wife", as Tuyu had been called. Here we come across a slight difficulty for Nefertiti calls her "nurse" or "tutor". Therefore, if Ay was Nefertiti's father, her mother must have been Ay's first wife, who died early on, leaving her in the charge of his second wife, Tey. This would certainly explain the title "nurse" which could mean stepmother. Ay was a man of great influence and importance in the Court of Akhenaten and if Nefertiti was not a foreign princess, which we can rightly suppose, we have to look for her father as a man of power and position. Such a man could only have been Ay. Compared to him, other men occupied only minor positions.

It is interesting at this stage, to review the state of the royal family. Amenophis III had married outside the dynastic family and then married his daughter. His son, unable to marry his sister, a daughter of the royal line, again married outside the royal family but only on the surface, for his wife, Nefertiti, was in fact the granddaughter of Tuyu and Yuya, his maternal grandparents. In other words he married his cousin. Nefertiti is recorded to have had six daughters, all of which are said to have been born by Year 9 of Akhenaten's reign. Merytaten, the eldest, married Smenkhkare and became Queen on his appointment as co-regent to Akhenaten.

She took the place of her mother shortly after Year 12, when Nefertiti is no longer mentioned, having either died at this time or disappeared from favour. Merytaten had a daughter, Merytaten-Tasherit, but little is known of her. Merytaten disappears from the scene quite soon, presumably having died before her husband. Nefertiti's second daughter, Meketaten, does not seem to have lived long after Year 12. The presence of Nefertiti in a painting on her tomb shows that when she died Nefertiti was still alive. Ankhesenpaaten who later became Ankhesenamun, a name we shall use for her throughout, was the third daughter of Nefertiti. She is important to us, for she became the wife of Tutankhamun. While still a princess she appears to have given birth to a daughter who was named after her, Ankhesenpaaten-Tasherit. Akhenaten is credited with being the father, but this is by no means certain.

Akhenaten as a person, is extremely mysterious and before continuing with our discussion of the intriguing relationships of this family, we must spend some time with this man who so completely upset Egyptian history. His very appearance as portrayed on the stone reliefs and statues is unusual to the point of being weird. Although we can perhaps explain some of the peculiarities away as artistic licence employed by the sculptors, anxious to experiment with new techniques during their newly found freedom of the period, it seems probable that they were in fact accurately portraying the peculiar physical features of this king. The break in artistic traditions allowed the sculptors to show things as they actually saw them, and not as convention demanded as in previous periods. Although Akhenaten was portrayed in the most peculiar compositions, and sometimes in the most unflattering of poses, he seems not to mind but encourage them. There can be no doubt that Akhenaten as a man had most peculiar features. He is shown with extremely large hips for a man, with feminine facial features, and sometimes with breasts. His head is elongated in the extreme, a feature which has been explained as hydrocephalus (an accumulation of fluid in the cranium, altering the shape of the skull). In fact, in many sculptures and reliefs he looks so much like a woman, that when divorced from their surroundings, it is difficult to say whether the figure is male or female.

Now, as we have said, the sculptors of this period were not shy at portraying all the peculiarities and ugliness of their subjects, in fact they were extremely honest observers. With this in mind, we must surely wonder when we see the remarkable colossal statue from the temple at Karnak, which shows the King completely naked, but without any genitals, a peculiarity that cannot be explained away as reluctance on the part of the sculptors to portray sexual organs. One is left wondering was there something wrong with him ? This is something surely that we must decide before discussing his relationship with other members of his family, especially his so-called descendants.

A number of suggestions have been put forward to explain away this peculiarity. Some have suggested that the Egyptians would not portray their King nude, a theory that must be overruled as there are other sculptures showing Pharaohs in the nude, although it must be admitted they are rare. Others have suggested that the statue may have been clothed, an unlikely answer, while others see in the statue some obscure religious ideal of bi-sexuality. Another point to note here, is that one of the titles of a Pharaoh, "The Strong Bull", implied he was a fertility king with strong semenal powers, and therefore a Pharaoh without a phallus contradicts this title. It is possible then, that Akhenaten was effeminate and may even have been a hermaphrodite. If he was, then he could not have been the father of Nefertiti's daughters.

Are we then to believe the evidence of the statues and conclude that there was even more intrigue in this incestuous family, or is there another explanation ? A theory which not only explains the peculiar sexual appearance of Akhenaten, but also the peculiar shape of his head, is that he was suffering from Fröhlich's syndrome, a condition usually caused by a tumour of the pituitary gland. This can cause abnormal physical characteristics to develop. The sexual organs in males may be so underdeveloped that they may be imbedded in fat and may not be visible. There is usually a build up of fat in the region of the breasts, abdomen, thighs, buttocks and pubis, giving a feminine appearance. Over-activity of the pituitary gland can also cause distortions of the skull, such as over growth of the jaw. This excessive functioning of the gland may then suddenly be followed by subnormal functioning. Fröhlich's syndrome usually cannot be diagnosed before puberty, the symptoms being almost a prolongation of puberty such as lack of body hair, infantile sexual organs and under-developed voice. Later, the female features such as breasts, buttocks and thighs appear. Occasionally this condition is accompanied by hydrocephalus. Hydrocephalus has been mentioned a number of times in connection with the physical characteristics of Akhenaten's head. This is strange, if we bear in mind the physical characteristics of his ancestors and his later relatives, who had rather exaggerated platycephalic (flat-headed) skulls.

Unfortunately we haven't yet discovered the mummy of Akhenaten and probably never will, or be able to decide the matter one way or the other.

If Akhenaten suffered from Fröhlich's disease, then we are still left with a problem, for he would be impotent and therefore could not have fathered Nefertiti's daughters, and we know from reliefs that she had six.

G   89

Whether he was a hermaphrodite or suffered from Fröhlich's syndrome he could not have been the father of his wife's children, that is if we are to believe the wealth of circumstantial evidence including the stone reliefs and statues. If Akhenaten did not father the children, who did ? We are led further into the depths of incestuous intrigue that permeated the Royal Court of the 18th Dynasty, for we are led to the possibility that Amenophis III was not adverse to sleeping with either his daughter, grand-daughter, or niece. Perhaps though, we are too harsh on him, for it must have been a heavy responsibility to find that his son was impotent, that the match he had made with a commoner at great risk, in an effort to continue the dynastic line should have come to such an end. No, he would have to see to it that Nefertiti did have children. Akhenaten, for his part, was only too willing to play in the charade, for on practically every relief he was shown as the family man with all his daughters. Remember too, that daughters were most important for dynastic succession. Some Egyptologists have always thought that Akhenaten made a little too much of a show about his family responsibilities, perhaps he doth protest too much.

All this may be speculation, but we have more evidence than just the reliefs, sculptures and medical prognosis. Unlike the daughters of other Pharaohs of the 18th Dynasty, who when depicted in reliefs or paintings were referred to simply as "Daughter of the King", none of the daughters of Akhenaten were ever shown with that epithet alone. Whenever any of the six Amarna princesses were depicted they were always accompanied by hieroglyphic inscriptions giving their titles and names as well as those of their mother Nefertiti. This is unusual because it is almost unique for the mother to be named, especially during the 18th Dynasty. It appears that every effort was made to ensure that there was no doubt as to who their mother was, but unfortunately there is every doubt as to who their father was. On no occasion does Akhenaten deliberately state that he was the father of the princesses. Up to now we have always assumed that Akhenaten was their father, as insinuated by the title "King's Daughter", but as we have seen on no occasion does he specifically state that he was their father, and, with the evidence available, we can seriously question this. There is an exception to this, however, as there is one case in which Akhenaten is referred to as the father of the first of the princesses, but this inscription is not in its original state, having been changed. Originally it referred to Nefertiti as wife of Akhenaten, but it was later changed to Merytaten wife of Akhenaten and the titles of the Queen were replaced with stock phrases referring to the princess, thus the connection is spurious and should be disregarded.

This uncertainty of the paternity of Nefertiti's daughters, also affects Ankhesenamun, or as she was called during the reign of Akhenaten, Ankhesenpaaten. Akhenaten has been accused of being the father of a daughter who was born to her, simply by an inscription that includes his name in close proximity, but the text is incomplete and it is not explicitly stated that he was the child's father. Merytaten, another of Nefertiti's daughters, also had a daughter, who is supposed to have been fathered by Akhenaten, but as she was the wife of Smenkhkare it seems more probable that he was the father. It seems strange that Akhenaten has been credited with fathering so many children, both daughters and grand-daughters, on such slender evidence. If we again refer to the sculptured reliefs for further clues, it is only because they provide much visual evidence. The relief in the tomb of Ay at Amarna, shows the palace harem of Akhenaten. It is a very accurate scene, showing all the various occupations of the inmates, from eating to preparing their toilet, and it is interesting to note that not a single child or baby is shown, a strange fact for the harem of a man so virile. He would surely have represented his numerous offspring on such a relief.

For further clues we must return again to the inscriptions referring to the daughters of Nefertiti. There is one scene in the tomb of Huya at Amarna, in which the princess Beketaten, accompanied by Queen Tiye is referred to as "King's daughter, of his loins, Beketaten". Inferring in this connection that her father was Amenophis III and her mother was Tiye. In the same relief other princesses of the royal family are referred to as "the King's daughter, of his loins, N. Born of the King's Chief Wife Nefertiti". The impression is given that the father remains the same, in this case Amenophis III, while the mothers differ, and one specifically identified in the inscription.

There is yet further circumstantial evidence which leads us to question the virility of Akhenaten. There is the strange affair between Smenkhkare and Akhenaten. Smenkhkare was appointed co-regent when Akhenaten was a relatively young man, certainly young enough, if he was able, to begat sons, and yet he took this unusual step of appointing Smenkhkare as co-regent. Why ? If he had had a son it would have caused a most embarrassing situation, for there is more to the affair than this. There are a number of reliefs showing the two monarchs together in compositions that can only be described as homosexual. If we add to this the fact that Smenkhkare incorporated into his cartouches the epithet "beloved of Akhenaten", and that he assumed the title of Nefertiti on her death, then we really have problems. Firstly it seems likely that Akhenaten was not the father of his wife's children, but that his father Amenophis III was; that he was in fact impotent, suffering from a disease that affected his sexual organs; and finally that

92

he preferred to have homosexual relations with his brother.

This is all of course conjecture. But conjecture based on evidence, the same sort of evidence on which most Egyptology is based. It depends on what one wants to believe. We can make him a saintly king, a religious fanatic, the original family man, or we can on the evidence available, question many peculiarities about this incredible man. A few years ago there were not many who would suggest this. Not because the evidence could not support it but that social stigmas attached to such things were just "not nice". The Egyptologist, Sir Alan Gardiner could not tolerate incestuous relationships in Egyptology and made every effort to interpret the evidence otherwise, although even he had to admit it took place occasionally.

The question of whether or not Akhenaten was the father of Nefertiti's children does affect our story, but only to a minor degree. Tutankhamun married Ankhesenamun, one of the daughters of Nefertiti, therefore if she was Akhenaten's daughter, Tutankhamun would have been related to Akhenaten as his son-in-law, but we will come to this again later.

We have mentioned several times the name of Smenkhkare as co-regent of Akhenaten, but who exactly was he ? The answer to this question is closely tied up with the identity of Tutankhamun. Some have suggested that Tutankhamun and Smenkhkare were outsiders, noblemen, not members of the royal family, who seized the throne through marriage to the daughters of the royal couple, Akhenaten and Nefertiti. With the discovery of the tomb of Tutankhamun, this theory cannot hold.

The identities of Smenkhkare and Tutankhamun are intimately linked, but in order to establish who Smenkhkare was, we have to start our investigation at tomb 55 in The Valley of the Kings. This was the tomb that we mentioned earlier had an important bearing on our story. Discovered in 1907 by Theodore Davis, almost opposite the site of the tomb of Tutankhamun, it contained a mummy in a damaged coffin. The identity of the occupant of the tomb has since been the subject of much speculation by numerous Egyptologists. The coffin posed a number of problems. Every effort had been made to erase the identity of the occupant. The name had been cut out of the coffin and the gold mummy bands, and the gold portrait mask removed.

The excavation that Davis carried out was slip-shod and the record was far from complete. Like that of Tutankhamun, the sealed doorway of this tomb also bore the seal of the royal necropolis, but Davis does not mention whether any other seals bearing the name of the occupant were found, we must therefore, on this incomplete evidence conclude, that either the burial was moved from elsewhere and re-sealed in tomb 55, or that Davis failed to notice or report the presence of any other seals. Further evidence which might have come from a foundation deposit was also overlooked. Therefore we can expect no clues of the royal occupant's identity from either door sealings or the foundation deposits.

The second doorway was found in a bad condition, and suggested that the tomb had been entered more than once. The contents were in disarray. In the corridor, part of a gilded shrine lay on its side, the other parts were in the large chamber at the end of the corridor. The woodwork was in an extremely fragile condition. The tomb was unfinished, the walls having been plastered but not painted. In the chamber, the coffin that had once rested on a bier lay broken on the floor, its lid off and the mummy exposed to the air. The bier had decomposed and collapsed, smashing the coffin to the ground and dislocating the lid. The sight was not an impressive one.

Among the contents of the chamber, was a set of alabaster Canopic jars, four "magic bricks" and numerous miscellaneous objects. Most important, though, were the names inscribed on the various pieces. The "magic bricks" had the name of Akhenaten, while a stone toilet vase bore the name of Amenophis III. Both Queen Tiye's and Amenophis III's names were inscribed on another, but the name of Amenophis III had later been erased. The name of Tutankhamun was also found inscribed on a number of small clay seals. A small stone amulet bore the name of Queen Tiye, while the figure of Tiye also appeared on the golden shrine together with her name and a donation inscription, which from its context implied the name Akhenaten, but whose name had been erased. In short every effort had been made throughout the tomb to remove the name of Akhenaten.

The climate then was rife for speculation, and heated arguments arose as to who the mummy was. Davis concluded that as the name of Queen Tiye was intact, the coffin was that of a woman, and the human heads on the lids of the Canopic jars found in a niche, appeared to him to be portraits of Queen Tiye; then the mummy was that of Queen Tiye. Davis also pointed out that the sheet gold headdress in the form of a vulture, found on the mummy, was a queen's crown and not one that would normally be worn by man. Others did not agree with him. In order to settle the matter Davis invited an American obstetrician who was visiting Thebes at the time, and a European doctor from Luxor, to examine the remains and determine the sex.

The body was in a delapidated condition and the mummy wrappings were badly decayed. The doctors had to lift them off in chunks, exposing the bones, all flesh having decomposed. After a quick examination, they are credited with an instant decision. They concluded the remains were those of a woman and justified their verdict by quoting the proportions of the pelvis, which in their opinion was all the proof that was needed. Davis, pleased with their report, promptly published his account of the discovery of "The Tomb of Queen Tiye", and that was that. But, that was not that, Egyptologists were not happy.

The mummy was sent to Cairo, where a further examination was conducted by the anatomist Professor G. Elliot Smith. The results of his examination completely contradicted the earlier report by the visiting American obstetrician. He found that the mummy was not that of an old woman, which he had expected, but of a young man, probably aged no more than twenty-three. Unfortunately, Elliot Smith became involved in the controversy and sought to establish that the body was that of Akhenaten. He was not very popular with some Egyptologists, who found it extremely difficult to fit in all the historical events of Akhenaten's reign into such a short life span. In order to appease them he put forward a number of suggestions to allow for the discrepancies, but they were not very convincing. He was, however, adamant that the bones were those of a man and not a woman, and because of the degree of epiphyseal union in the long bones, and other similar anatomical evidence, it was unlikely that they belonged to a person older than twenty-five. His examination was mainly concerned in determining the age and sex of the individual and he did not at first go into the details of Akhenaten's peculiar features, though he did suggest that the cranium showed signs of chronic hydrocephalus. Later he made some attempt at explaining the peculiar anatomical features shown in contemporary artistic representations of Akhenaten with his anatomical observations, by suggesting the possibility of Fröhlich's syndrome.

In 1931, Dr. Derry who had earlier conducted the anatomical examination of the mummy of Tutankhamun, re-examined the remains from tomb 55. He disagreed with Elliot Smith and claimed that the skull did not show signs of hydrocephalus, and was not abnormal, although it was of unusual shape. He pointed out that it was very similar to that of Tutankhamun. He however, agreed with Professor Smith on the age of the individual, confirming that the body was of a young man of not more than twenty-three years of age. He suggested that the occupant of tomb 55 was in fact Smenkhkare, a view first put forward by the Egyptologists Norman Davies and Kurt Gethe.

The coffin still posed a few problems. Everyone now agreed that the mummy was of a young man and yet the coffin appeared to be made for a young woman. In 1916 the French scholar, Georges Daressy had suggested that the coffin was made for a woman, probably Queen Tiye, and had later been altered for a king. During the restoration of the coffin at the Cairo Museum, Rex Engelbach made a thorough study of the coffin and concluded that it had been made for Smenkhkare before he was king, and later modified for him when he was crowned.

The controversy has continued up to recent times, for in 1957 Sir Alan Gardiner published a study of the coffin text and asserted that the coffin had belonged to Akhenaten, or was thought to belong to him. Other Egyptologists disagreed and pointed out that the coffin was made for a woman, probably Merytaten, the wife of Smenkhkare. Opinions on the identity of the mummy, however, continued to differ, the names of both Akhenaten and Smenkhkare being suggested. It was obvious that the matter could only be resolved by a new and thorough clinical examination of the remains using modern techniques.

Such an examination was carried out in 1963 by Professor H. G. Harrison of Liverpool University and Professors Batrani and Mahmoud of Cairo. And now after all these years we have the answer.

The results were extremely interesting and very illuminating. Not only do we know how old the occupant was at death, and the sex, but also we now have an accurate idea of the physical features and peculiarities.

Professor Harrison's most detailed report is a landmark in the anatomical examinations of Egyptian mummies. He concluded that the remains were those of a young man, under twenty-five years old and about 5 feet 7 inches tall. Using anatomical evidence such as the detailed assessment of epiphyses of various bones, the state of the symphyseal surface of the pubis and the degree of wear on the teeth, he suggested it was possible to be more definite about the time of death, and placed it about the twentieth year.

He paid special attention to the skull and decided that there was no evidence of hydrocephalus, he also excluded the possibility of a pituitary tumour, and pointed out that the proportions of the body were normal and showed no signs of endocrinopathies (malfunction of the endocrine glands). The remains also showed minimal signs of hypogonadism and eunochoidism. He did, however, point out that the remains showed some female traits but the individual would be a normal male. Having obtained this valuable information, the Professors decided to attempt a reconstruction of the contour of the head and face on the skull. This can be done using a known formula, whereby the maximum and minimum thickness of flesh at twenty three points are utilised to build up a three dimensional likeness. The work was carried out by Mr. D. J. Kidd, Medical Artist to the Faculty of Medicine, University of Liverpool. The results were surprising to the point of being startling.

The portrait bore a striking resemblance to Tutankhamun as depicted on his mummiform coffins. At no stretch of the imagination could it be compared with the portraits of Akhenaten, as shown on the stone reliefs. The drawing was completely unbiased, as Mr. Kidd had not seen portraits of either Smenkhkare or Akhenaten, and in addition had no idea of the identity of the remains on which he was working. Another interesting point was that his portrait bore no resemblance to a sculpture in the Louvre in Paris, which has often been suggested to be that of Smenkhkare.

It is interesting that the relationship between the two mummies was first noticed by Dr. Derry, the doctor who had carried out the anatomical examination of Tutankhamun in 1925 and later the examination of the remains of tomb 55. He published a comparative table of anatomical measurements in his report on Tutankhamun's mummy, in Howard Carter's "The Tomb of Tutankhamen." Dr. Harrison pointed out that not only were the measurements similar, but there was also great similarity in the width between the angles of the mandibles (lower jaw bone).

The most obvious conclusion to draw from all this evidence is that the occupant of tomb 55 was closely related to Tutankhamun, and they were most probably brothers.

Further conclusive evidence was provided in 1969, when using techniques recently developed in the Department of Anatomy, University of Liverpool, Professor Harrison and Dr. R. C. Connolly carried out a serological analysis on the remains from tomb 55 and those of Tutankhamun. This extremely ingenious micromethod could detect specific blood group substances. In the case of Tutankhamun only about 10 mg. of tissue dust was used. The principle of the test was based on the fact that ABH blood group substances occur widely in the body as well as in the red blood corpuscles. Their nature is such that they tend to survive both climate and microbile degradation, and can therefore even be detected in ancient human remains. The MN antigens also appear to survive, but not the antigens of the Rhesus system. The results of the tests show that both Tutankhamun and the occupant of tomb 55 belong to blood group A2 and they were both MN.

If the occupant of tomb 55 was so closely related to Tutankhamun, was of such a young age, and buried in such a manner, the circumstances point to the occupant being Smenkhkare.

Thus we have established not only the identity of the occupant of tomb 55, but also the relationship between Tutankhamun and Smenkhkare. Now we must try to establish the parentage of these two brothers. To do this we must look at the funerary furniture of Tutankhamun, which provides us with the best clues. We have already mentioned the suggestion by some Egyptologists, that the two kings were simply influential nobles who had become Pharaohs by marrying princesses. As we can see from the mummy of Tutankhamun, this is impossible as he would have only been about nine years old at the time of his succession, and one could hardly see a child of that age making the subtle political moves necessary for such an act. The relationship between Tutankhamun and Smenkhkare also makes nonsense of this suggestion. In fact, if they were brothers as we can assume they were, then it would be acceptable for Tutankhamun to succeed his brother. We must also come back again to the fact that Akhenaten does not seem to have had any sons. If this is so, it would then not be unusual for him to appoint a close relation to the position of co-regent. It could be suggested, as some have, that Smenkhkare was Akhenaten's son, but the evidence does not support this. Such a close anatomical relationship between Smenkhkare and Tutankhamun, would suggest that they had the same mother. Such a woman would have to be a very important person, and one of high rank in the royal harem. This could not have been Nefertiti, for she is always shown with daughters, never sons, and Akhenaten would have been the first one to have them portrayed had she had any.

It was the normal practice in the 18th Dynasty for the eldest son to marry the royal heiress on his succession as co-regent, which occurred when he reached manhood, or if he came to the throne before reaching maturity, he was married to the royal heiress and would father children as soon as he reached the age of puberty. In either case Akhenaten could not be the father of Smenkhkare, as he ruled for only seventeen years and Smenkhkare, who is thought to have died at almost the same time, was aged about twenty.

So we now have two brothers, presumably of royal parentage, who became Pharaohs of Egypt, succeeding Akhenaten. Who then was their father? Tutankhamun had inscribed on a granite statue of a lion, a declaration in which he explicitly calls Amenophis III his father. He had found the sculpture lying unfinished in a quarry on his succession, and had it completed and installed in the temple of Amenophis III at Sulb. It is interesting that little attention was paid to this statue until recent times. Some Egyptologists preferred to see the inscription as an attempt by Tutankhamun to claim grand parentage, while others saw it as meaning forefather and not literally father. Bearing this inscription in mind, we must now examine the evidence of Tutankhamun's funerary furniture.

Probably the most important clue was a little gold statue of Amenophis III, which had been worn by Tutankhamun on a chain and which was buried with him enclosed in two miniature coffins, an object treated with great reverence as a family heirloom. Also in Tutan-khamun's tomb, and treated with similar reverence, was a plaited lock of Queen Tiye's auburn hair enclosed in a sarcophagus, discovered beside the gold figure of Amenophis III.

Apart from the little statue, there were other objects found in the tomb bearing the name of Amenophis III, including an alabaster pitcher with the names of both Amenophis III and Tiye. The overwhelming weight of evidence implies that Tutankhamun and Smenkhkare were both the sons of Tiye and Amenophis III, and were in fact the brothers of Akhenaten and not his sons. We can be fairly sure that their mother was Tiye for the gold portrait mask of Tutankhamun bore a remarkable resemblance to a carved ebony head of Queen Tiye. We know that Tiye was of child-bearing age in the 39th regnal year of Amenophis III, when she gave birth to Beketaten. It therefore seems reasonable that Tutan-khamun was born to her about the 7th-8th regnal year of Akhenaten, having previously given birth to Smenkh-kare in about the 24th regnal year of Amenophis III. Why then were these two sons kept such a secret? Perhaps it wasn't such a secret for as we have already said, it became the practice under Amenophis III to stress the importance of royal daughters, and therefore only royal daughters were portrayed.

Having now established the identity of Tutankhamun and Smenkhkare, we can begin to understand their positions in the peculiar events which followed the accession of Akhenaten. It must have been all too clear to Akhenaten that he could not father a son, not even with the help of Amenophis III and so the logical thing for him to do would be to appoint his brother as co-regent. It would then follow that the children of Smenkhkare, under normal circumstances, would have been in line of succession, but as Merytaten, Smenkhkare's wife died early, as had his only daughter, he died without leaving any heirs. Therefore the throne came to Tutankhamun, who could justly claim his right as Pharaoh as the son of Amenophis III, married to the daughter of a Pharaoh, Ankhesenamun.

CHAPTER TEN

★

INTRIGUE

The events which governed the life of Tutankhamun began almost seven years before he was born. Amenophis III, who had already ruled for about twenty-nine years, took as his co-regent his son Akhenaten, who at this time was still known as Amenophis IV. From the very beginning Akhenaten allowed his overwhelming interest in theology to rule his actions. The religious situation that Akhenaten inherited was extremely complex. A number of religious beliefs and doctrines existed, which entailed the worship of a vast pantheon of gods and goddesses, who themselves had numerous forms, both animal and human.

The prehistoric fertility cults, entailing the worship of the cow as the provider of mankind, and the bull or ram as the fertility symbol still survived; to which were added religious ideas based upon the natural cycle of regeneration of the soil by the Nile. An Egyptian creation legend grew out of this idea. The legend goes that the flood waters of the Nile receded, exposing small mounds of dry land here and there. The god incarnate alighted as a bird, sometimes a falcon, other times an ibis, and yet others as a phoenix. Vegetation sprouted and animal life flourished, feeding off the vegetation and each other. Thus life began out of chaos. Each year the Nile would rise flooding the land and creating chaos, which receding would leave fertile soil to grow the crops, a resurrection of the land from the life-giving waters, and an idea to inspire a cosmogeny.

To these primeval ideas were added two other sources of religious beliefs. One, the belief in the universal sky god, manifest as a falcon, Horus; the Pharaoh as the god incarnate. The other and more important was the worship of the sun, this was more sophisticated than the other beliefs and was a much later development. The sun-god, Re-Atum, had his city at Heliopolis and was considered the creator of the universe. The Pharaoh was not in this case the god incarnate but was considered his son, the god assuming the form of the Pharaoh to marry the Chief Queen, therefore, her son would be the son of the god.

Horus the falcon was the god of the sky, but he was also worshipped by the followers of Re-Atum, as he bore on his wings the sun-disc, which he carried across the heavens. The Pharaoh, as the incarnation of Horus, was also the son of the sun-god. An ancient fertility god, Osiris, was at one time killed, dismembered, and his remains buried and dedicated to the greater fertility of the land. The Pharaoh as Horus incarnate became Osiris at death, his remains buried as Osiris for the greater fertility and benefit of the land. The new Horus took his place, thus the worship of Osiris also became linked with the worship of the sun. All these beliefs combined with each other and interacted, and it is almost impossible to separate them.

By the time of his accession to the throne, Akhenaten's thoughts had already progressed to the worship of one god, in preference to the multitude of gods which proliferated Egyptian religion. His ideas were based on the already existing ideology of sun worship, but he altered the conception to an abstract ideal of which the sun-disc, the Aten, was the visible element. This rather general description of Akhenaten's religious ideas, may seem to us today as rather mild. However, at the time and in the background of ancient Egyptian religious thought, such ideas were in themselves a heresy of paramount importance. The whole of the Egyptian State was intimately and inextricably connected with religion. Politics and religion were one and the same. A change in religious thought, therefore, was also a change in political thought.

The importance of the sun god, the Aten, had already been growing earlier during the 18th Dynasty, and Amenophis III himself had dedicated his State barge to the Aten in about his 11th regnal year, by naming it 'Radiance of the Aten'. He also included the name of Aten in the name of his two children, Princess Beketaten and Prince Tutankhaten (later Tutankhamun). The main difference, however, between the position of Aten before the accession of Akhenaten was that it fitted into the vast pantheon of gods, whereas under Ankhenaten it became the supreme deity and the only deity which he recognised. It was this unique feature of Akhenaten's thinking that separates him and establishes him as one of the foremost philosophers and theologians of the ancient world. Such thinking was revolutionary and far in advance of its time, and as such was to prove unacceptable to the Egyptian people. In time it was to bring about not only the downfall of Akhenaten himself but also of the dynastic family.

For us to fully understand the seriousness of his religious ideals, we must examine the position of the Pharaoh in Egypt at this time. We have already seen how his father, Amenophis III, had flaunted religious tradition by marrying outside the dynastic family, and explained the religious and political implications of his act.

In Egypt the Pharaoh was supreme. The entire land

and resources, men and animals belonged to him. He was on equal terms with the gods and greater than mortal, and acted as intermediary between the gods and men. The people regarded him as a god, and his thoughts and pronouncements were oracular. It was the Pharaoh who dedicated and founded temples, and donated lands and revenues for their upkeep. In return, the gods gave him universal domination as ruler of Egypt and lord of all nations, by divine right.

In archaic times, the Pharaoh was considered as the incarnation of the falcon headed god, Horus, a supreme universal sky god, whose title was conferred upon the King as the Living Horus. Later, with the growth of the worship of the sun god, Re-Atum, the Pharaoh was regarded as the son of Re, but still acknowledged as the Living Horus. During the 18th Dynasty the position of the Pharaoh was even greater, rising to a peak under Amenophis III, who was worshipped as a god and in one or two temple reliefs is shown worshipping himself. Thus, Akhenaten could with little difficulty, both as political and religious head of State and controller of revenue, alter religious ideas simply by diverting revenues from the temples of other gods to his own, and then ignoring all others except the Aten. This although slightly over-simplified, is exactly what he did.

As we have already seen, Akhenaten on his accession to the throne as co-regent to his father, already had firm ideas on monotheism, and with his new found power as Pharaoh, set out to put his ideas into practice. He had to be cautious as he was not sole ruler but joint ruler, and had to respect to a certain degree the wishes and beliefs of his father, Amenophis III, who had his court at Malkata, Thebes, whose city god was Amun. However cautious, this did not deter him from establishing the supremacy of the Aten, and we may even suspect that Amenophis III himself was in sympathy with his son's ideas, although not in a position to express them himself.

During the first few years of Akhenaten's reign, established sun deities such as Re-Herakhty, a combination of the sun god Re, with the sky god Horus, were raised to a high position. Re is established as supreme divine power, displacing Amun. Re being manifest in the light of the Disc. Later the Aten, as a heavenly king, is established and represented by the rayed sun disc, developed from the hieroglyph for sun-shine. The Disc replaced the old anthropomorphic and therianthropic forms. The rays from the Disc ended in the form of hands, which sometimes held the sign of life, the Ankh, but only to the King and Queen. An inscription on the ceiling of Tutankhamun's third shrine gives the meaning of the rays,

"The rays of the Aten are as a protection over thee, their hands possessing health and life. They are to thee as prosperity to thy members"

The name of the Aten was enclosed in a cartouche and treated as a heavenly Pharaoh. Akhenaten regarded himself not only as the son of the Aten but also as his co-regent. Thus his position appears even more secure than his predecessors as 'Sons of Re', in that he was co-regent with a heavenly Pharaoh. He also returned to early ideas, re-establishing the belief that all offerings and prayers to the god could only be made through him.

During the seven years before Tutankhamun's birth, the basis of the heresy had been firmly established by Akhenaten. After his coronation, Akhenaten would have set up his separate and independent Court at Thebes. His first act to establish the supremacy of his god, the Aten, was to enlarge the already existing shrine 'The Mansion of Aten' at Karnak, which stood east of the temple of Amun. The temple of the Aten was to be of gigantic proportions, and to build it he had to open a new quarry at Gebel Silsileh to extract sandstone. He commemorated the opening of the quarry by erecting a stela on which he is described as being a high priest of Re-Herakhty. The temple of the Aten at Karnak shows the new art style which developed to express the new religious ideas, the new "truth" in art. This new art form, known to us as "Amarna", was a renaissance of Egyptian art. Great freedom was allowed the sculptors, who took the opportunity to experiment with forms and techniques, which under the old conservative ideals could not possibly have been allowed to be executed. The result was a form of expressionism unparalleled to the present day. Portraits of Royalty are humanised and natural peculiarities faithfully shown and sometimes almost exaggerated. The period of the Amarna art style unfortunately did not survive long after Akhenaten's death, when Egyptian artistic ideals reverted to the conservatism of former times.

The building of the temple of the Aten at Karnak was only the first step. It was obvious that the Aten would have to be established in his own city, as were the other gods of ancient Egypt. Akhenaten soon found a site, about mid-way between Memphis and Thebes. Here he built Akhetaten, "The Horizon of Aten", which is present day Tell el-Amarna. He asserted that the Aten himself had chosen the site, and that as it belonged to no god, goddess or man, he would build there the city of the Aten. It is possible that as early as Year 4 of his reign he had dedicated a preliminary boundary stone. The inscription on the stone gives us a good picture of the foundation ceremony. The King, in his electrum plated State chariot rode to a large altar where offerings and ceremonies took place. Everyone was there, courtiers, state officials, officers of the army, all paying homage to Akhenaten while he addressed them, stating that it was the Aten himself who had chosen the site. The gathering on hearing this, vouched that all nations would come to Akhetaten and pay tribute to the Aten, and that they understood that the Aten would only make known his wishes to his son, Akhenaten. Akhenaten then swore an oath, raising his hands to the Sun Disc, saying that he would only build Akhetaten for his father, the Aten, there and nowhere else, and named the buildings he intended to erect in the city. There would be a "Mansion of the Aten", a "House of the Aten", a "Sunshade of the Queen", and a "House of Rejoicing for the Aten in the Island", together with apartments for the Pharaoh and the Queen. He vowed that all members of the royal family and high officials would be buried at Akhetaten, and stated that he would make arrangements for tombs to be hewn out of the cliffs in the eastern mountains, for himself, his wife Nefertiti, and her daughter Merytaten.

Work on the city progressed and about Year 5 to 6 Akhenaten moved with his Court to Akhetaten. In Year 6 he changed his name from Amenophis IV to Akhenaten. Also in that year, he dedicated another boundary stone at Akhetaten, on the second anniversary of the founding of the city. On this occasion he fixed the boundaries of the city within accurate dimensions. This was essential for taxation purposes, for all property and revenue within the boundaries was dedicated to the Aten. The scene must have been similar to the foundation ceremony conducted two years previous, with Akhenaten riding in his golden State chariot to the boundaries of the city. At each point he made an oath that he would not pass beyond the boundary of the new city. The measurements on the stelae maintain that Akhetaten extended from north to south for nearly eight miles, with a similar distance on the west. Everything within this area belonged to the Aten, the mountains, the fields, the deserts, the farmland, the water, the animals and men and women.

The mention of the oath of Akhenaten, not to leave the boundaries of Akhetaten, has led to the impression that he did not leave the city. This, however, is extremely improbable, and is contradicted by a number of inscriptions which state that if Akhenaten or any member of his family were to die outside Akhetaten, they were to be brought back to the city for burial. In fact, it was the practice in ancient Egypt, for the Pharaoh and his Court to travel the land and to stay at the palaces at such centres as Memphis and Thebes.

We see then, that Akhenaten changed his name and moved to his City of the Aten about the 33rd or 34th regnal year of his father, Amenophis III, the year of his second Jubilee. Also in this year Akhenaten changed his name from Amenophis IV, and added to the name of his wife, Nefertiti, the title "Nefer-neferu-Aten", "Fair is the Goodness of the Aten". He also changed the title of the Aten, whom he called "The Father Divine and Royal, who is in Jubilees and is in the House of the Aten at Akhetaten". This happened two years before the birth of Tutankhamun.

When Akhenaten first came to the throne, he had to establish a separate Court and would have needed skilled officials and scribes. These he mostly recruited from the sons of the officials in the Court of his father at Malkata, as it was the practice in ancient Egypt for the eldest son to succeed to his father's job. Thus, the establishment of a separate Court would provide unparelleled opportunities. It is now that we first see the growing influence and importance of Ay, who as "Father of the God", (the father of Nefertiti) had also assumed the title of his father, Yuya, as "Master of the Horse". He was both military commander and State adviser and held great sway with the King. Although outside the

111

dynastic family proper, we have seen that he was related to Akhenaten both as father-in-law and as uncle, his sister being Queen Tiye. Akhenaten had a fine tomb hewn at Akhetaten for Ay, and it is in this tomb that one of the best preserved inscriptions of the "Hymn to the Aten" can be found. Ay, however, was never buried there, and it is extremely doubtful whether he paid more than lip service to the worship of the Aten. He seems to have been a career man, dedicated not so much to the Pharaoh, but to the Empire of Egypt itself, and was therefore only interested in its wellbeing. In his position, however, he could only advise the King, who it seems often chose to ignore his advice, his thoughts and actions clouded by religious ideologies. We should always remember that Ay's elder brother, Anen, held a high position in the hierachy at Thebes during the reign of Akhenaten's father, Amenophis III. He was Greatest of Seers in the temple of Re-Atum, and the Second of the Four Chief Prophets of Amun. It is therefore interesting, that while Ay served Akhenaten and the Aten, his brother served Amenophis III and the god Amun.

Thus, in the eight years before Tutankhamun's birth, the stage had already been set for the events that were to follow during his lifetime. Tutankhamun was probably born to Tiye, the Chief Queen of Amenophis III, at the Malkata Palace at Thebes, in the 36th regnal year of his father, Amenophis III. At his birth, he was not in direct line of succession and under normal circumstances would not have attained the throne, were it not for the peculiar events that were to follow. His father, Amenophis III, was still reigning at Thebes, while his brother, Akhenaten, had already been co-regent for eight years and his Court established at Akhetaten for two years. It therefore followed that should Akhenaten have had sons and daughters, the succession would not have come his way, and even if Akhenaten did not have heirs,

Tutankhamun had an elder brother, Smenkhkare, who was already about thirteen years old at the time of Tutankhamun's birth. Akhenaten's wife, Nefertiti, did have daughters. One of them, Ankhesenpaaten (later Ankhesenamun) had been born before Tutankhamun and was to become his wife. Tutankhamun was the last child of Tiye and Amenophis III.

At the time of his birth, the affairs of Egypt were already becoming chaotic, in spite of the fact that his father still reigned at Thebes. Akhenaten was becoming increasingly obsessed with his religious ideals, and although it would have been his job as younger Pharaoh to have maintained Egypt's boundaries, he took little interest in foreign affairs. His lack of interest in foreign affairs continued throughout his reign and was to cause the loss of a number of Egypt's vassal states. In fact, after the tribute of Year 12, foreign princes largely chose to ignore him, sending only sporadic gifts, and eventually ceasing to send them altogether.

Tutankhamun would have spent the first few years of his life in the care of his mother, Tiye, at the Malkata Court at Thebes. His brother, Smenkhkare, would probably have resided at Memphis, the seat of the next in line of succession. He must have moved there when he was about five years old, on the accession of his brother as co-regent to his father. He would not, however, have expected to succeed to the throne, as it would have been more than likely that his brother would produce heirs of his own. Tutankhamun would have been too young to have noticed the state of confusion that was gradually growing in the Malkata Court. It was obvious to the old officials and the priests of Amun, that Akhenaten had no interest in the god Amun or his city, Thebes, and that as their Pharaoh, Amenophis III was getting old it seemed inevitable that Thebes would shortly fall on lean times. This to a conservative people would have been most disturbing. The population too, although used to obeying the oracular thoughts of their Pharaoh, must have wondered at the strange new thoughts of Akhenaten, and although outwardly prepared to accept the new ideas, inwardly they were probably disconcerted, and privately cherished the old beliefs.

Shortly after his first birthday, Tutankhamun was taken by his mother, Tiye, along with his father to Akhetaten, on the occasion of his father's third Jubilee. Akhenaten had built a residence for his father, as well as his mother and his sister Beketaten, and it is probable that Tutankhamun spent periods here from time to time, in between his stays at Malkata. At Akhetaten work proceeded almost at a feverish pace. Akhenaten had to make do with few experienced workmen or overseers, as the majority were still employed by the old King at Thebes, where building operations still continued. This did not deter Akhenaten, however, who employed large numbers of inexperienced workers. Gradually the city took shape; it was well laid out and must have been very fine indeed.

The first area to be constructed was the South City, which contained the residences of important officials. The King had a Pleasure Palace here, Maru-Aten, with lakes, pools and coloured pavements, and the Sunshade Temples or kiosks dedicated to the Queen and princesses. The North Suburb contained the houses of the merchant class and lesser officials, the houses being smaller and less salubrious. It was probably here, that the agricultural produce from across the river on the west bank, was landed at the quays. Here also were the slums of the poor. To the north was the Northern City of which we know little. The Central City was the official area, containing the large palace and other major official buildings. The palace extended nearly half a mile along the large thoroughfare known today as Sikket es-

Sultan, the King's way, and westwards down to the river bank. Around the palace were other official buildings and temples, such as the Great Temple on its northern boundary and the Small Temple on its southern side. These temples were gigantic, the Great Temple covering an area of approximately 200,000 square yards and the Small Temple with an area of 25,000 square yards. Nearby were the police quarters and "the House of Correspondence of the Pharaoh". Although lavishly planned there was no system of drainage. The majority of the domestic buildings were constructed of mud brick, sometimes coated with plaster and sometimes painted in colours. The large buildings had stone door-posts, lintels, column bases, etc., while the temples and major parts of the palace were constructed of limestone, enhanced with alabaster, quartzite, and granite. Much of the decoration of the palace and temple walls was in coloured inlays of stone and glazed tiles. Unlike the temples of Amun, which gradually got darker as one progressed towards the inner sanctum, the temples of the Aten were large open courtyards exposed to the rays of the sun, in which large numbers of mud altars stood on which offerings were made to the Aten.

By Year 9 of Akhenaten's reign, both the Central and Southern sections of the city had been completed. Also in Year 9, Akhenaten again changed the names of the Aten to accord with his evolved thinking. This time he called the Aten "Re the Living, the Ruler of the Horizon, who Rejoices on the Horizon", and "in his manifestation of Re-the-Father, who Returns as the Sun-Disc". The Aten was also known as "Lord of Jubilees".

By this time, news of the activities of the young King at Akhetaten must have spread throughout the Empire. Strange stories of his ideas and of the queer new art forms that were developed there, must have been told by the hordes of menials that accompanied both

Akhenaten and his father, Amenophis III, on their travels to various palaces in Egypt. Foreign kings too, were aware of what was going on and were addressing some of their correspondence to the elder King, Amenophis III, at Akhetaten, as early as Year 36 of his reign. During this time Akhenaten could do little permanent damage, as his father still supported the priests of Amun; but on his death events accelerated and the real damage began to be done.

The old King, Amenophis, died in about his 39th to 40th regnal year, when Tutankhamun was about three or four. Although of tender age, he would have attended the lavish funeral ceremonies at Thebes, which his brother carried out according to custom. Amenophis was buried in the western branch of The Valley of the Kings. The news spread beyond the boundaries of Egypt, and at Thebes, Akhenaten received a letter of condolence from the King of Mitanni. On Akhenaten's return to Akhetaten, he held a large and sumptuous ceremony at which he and his Queen, Nefertiti, received tribute from foreign rulers, in recognition of his succession as sole ruler. This was in his 12th regnal year.

The life of the young Tutankhamun must have been turned almost upside-down by the death of his father. For now Akhenaten could direct the entire revenue, originally allocated to the temples of Amun at Thebes, to his own at Akhetaten. He completely ignored Amun and all the other gods. Thus, with Thebes stripped of its position, the importance of Akhetaten was secure. Tutankhamun would have moved with his mother, Tiye, and his sister, Beketaten, to their residence at Akhetaten. Whereas the world at Thebes revolved around Amun, his world now at Akhetaten, revolved around the Aten. This change, although great, could not have affected him a great deal but the events which were to follow in the next few years certainly did. A series of unfortunate incidents occurred after the death of Amenophis III, which seem to have had a great effect on the mental stability of Akhenaten, whose pacifist policy of ignoring the other gods turned to one of vengeance.

All the reliefs show him as a devout family man, usually with his wife, Nefertiti, and her daughters. From all accounts he appears to have been most attached to her and when she died, sometime after Year 12, he was strongly affected by her loss. Her daughter, Merytaten, took her place. Shortly before the death of Nefertiti, her daughter Meketaten had also died. Thus, within a short period, he suffered the loss of his father, his wife and her daughter. He had no male heirs, and with the death of his father and his wife he knew he could not hope for a successor, who would appear to the populace as a continuation of his branch of the dynastic family. There was no use in marrying afresh as he could not procreate children. Therefore, although some Egyptologists have suggested that Merytaten, his daughter, bore him a child, the father almost certainly was Smenkhkare.

It was now, with his mind almost certainly unhinged by personal loss, that he hit out at the other gods. Surely it was not the Aten that had let him down, but the fact that the other gods were worshipped in a land that belonged to the Aten ? He struck out viciously against the other cults, especially that of Amun. Between Tutankhamun's fifth and ninth birthdays, he must have witnessed strange scenes, with artisans hacking out the names of the god Amun from statues and inscriptions, and even from the name of Akhenaten's father himself. The temples of Amun at Thebes were desecrated and burned, and statues of the god Amun destroyed. Akhenaten's fanatical hatred of Amun was directed on objects as large as a temple or as small as a scarab, on which the name of Amun was inscribed. He also caused all reference to the plural of god to be erased from

117

monuments and inscriptions. All this took a great deal of time, and Tutankhamun must have watched in bewilderment as he grew up at Akhetaten, and when he was taken on occasional trips to Thebes and Memphis.

These activities must have worried the statesman Ay, who could see the effect on his beloved Egypt. Whereas he was quite willing to pay lip service to the Aten, he was unwilling to see the destruction of Egypt through the megalomania of one man. But events were not to stop here. Realizing that he had no heir to offer Egypt, Akhenaten appointed his brother, Smenkhkare, co-regent, when Tutankhamun was about six years old. The scenes at Akhetaten must have been really weird on occasions. Tutankhamun would witness scenes where the two brothers, Smenkhkare and Akhenaten, acted more like man and wife than co-regents. They continually appeared in public in situations which can only be regarded as homosexual. Akhenaten's physical peculiarities seemed to have affected his psychological sexual appetite, preferring homosexual relationships. His brother seems to have been of similar mind for he appears to have openly participated. Akhenaten conferred upon Smenkhkare the titles of his beloved Nefertiti. From all appearances Smenkhkare seems to have been effeminate, although only in actions and not physically, as we have seen from his mummy. Perhaps he only went along with Akhenaten out of brotherly love, unfortunately we shall never know.

Merytaten was married to Smenkhkare and he set up his own Court. Although he established himself at Thebes, he spent much of his time at Akhetaten, where both he and Akhenaten must have come into constant contact with the young Tutankhamun. During this time, Tutankhamun still lived with his mother Tiye, who must have watched with growing horror the activities of her two sons. At Thebes, the young Smenkhkare may have made a feeble effort to placate the city god Amun, but he appeared to have held sympathy with the Aten. Thus the priests of Amun could expect no help from him and Egypt seemed doomed to continual chaos.

Akhenaten seemed quite happy with his homosexual relationship with his brother, and encouraged sculptors to portray the two monarchs in homosexual scenes. Perhaps to him, he was acting out an obscure religious thought with himself as the god figure. With the death of Smenkhkare's wife, Merytaten, the situation became acute. All Egypt was talking about the strange happenings and the old Queen Tiye herself, must have done her utmost to see that the young Tutankhamun did not follow in the footsteps of his two brothers. It is possible that Ay, seeing both the calamitous state of Egypt's boundaries and imminent internal disorder caused by the two monarchs' actions, had consultations with his sister, the dowager Queen Tiye, seeking a solution. To him it seemed the only possible solution was to place the young Tutankhamun on the throne. To do this he would have to remove both Akhenaten and Smenkhkare. He could not afford to take the risk of leaving Smenkhkare on the throne, as he had openly collaborated with his brother Akhenaten and would probably follow similar policies if he became sole ruler. It was also possible that Smenkhkare would be unpopular with the people and foreign rulers. This must have alarmed Queen Tiye, who, although concerned about the state of Egypt, could not condone the murder of her two sons, for murder it would have to be, for there was no other way. Ay therefore had to bide his time.

Tiye died about the 16th to 17th regnal year of Akhenaten, the 2nd to 3rd regnal year of Smenkhkare. Shortly after her death, both Smenkhkare and Akhenaten died mysteriously and almost simultaneously. However, Smenkhkare died first, and Akhenaten, who was stricken with grief, had his mummy bound and arranged as a woman. Tutankhamun was married to Nefertiti's daughter, Ankhesenamun, and according to the ancient traditions, succeeded to the throne of Egypt.

CHAPTER ELEVEN

★

MURDER

Whether Ay carried out his plan, or whether providence intervened and arranged the miraculous deaths of the two monarchs, we do not know. Whether natural or not, their deaths were most timely and saved Egypt from sinking into greater depths of disorder.

The task in front of Tutankhamun on his accession to the throne was daunting. But perhaps we should say the task facing Ay, for at the tender age of nine, Tutankhamun was in no position to put the country in order or to exercise his will. He was in the position of a puppet ruler, the real power being in the hands of his uncle, Ay, and it is now that we begin to see the statesmanship of Ay in action.

Ay was careful to ensure that Tutankhamun would be acceptable to the people as legitimate ruler. Tutankhamun's marriage to a royal princess was in accordance with custom, and not only confirmed his right to the throne in the eyes of the people, but also in the eyes of the traditional chief god, Amun. Also according to tradition, Tutankhamun was crowned Pharaoh by the priests of Amun, as custom prescribed, in the temples at Memphis and later at Thebes.

At the time of his accession to the throne, Tutankhamun was still called by his Atenist name, Tutankhaten, as was his wife, Ankhesenpaaten. Both resided at Akhetaten, probably in the old residence of Nefertiti. Ay did not react violently against the Aten, to do so would have created even greater disorder. His plan was gradually to remove the influence of the heresy, slowly erasing it from people's memories. So although no direct action was taken against the Aten, he liberalised religious thought by encouraging the worship of the other gods, especially Amun. After a while Akhetaten was abandoned by Tutankhamun and his Court, and they moved to Memphis and Thebes. He never went back to Akhetaten, which was gradually abandoned and the city fell into decay. Most of Tutankhamun's furniture and belongings were taken by river to his palaces at Thebes and Memphis, some of which was buried with him in his tomb.

It was now official policy to allow the worship of all the gods and although the worship of the Aten was quietly dropped, Tutankhamun, it seems, was still a believer and continued to worship the Aten, although probably in private. We can see evidence of this on much of the furniture from his tomb, which is in the Amarna art style, and which is inscribed with the name of the Aten. From the age of the King and Queen, as depicted on the golden throne, we can see that he still worshipped the Aten when in his teens. This must have alarmed Ay, who was doing everything in his power to erase the memory of the Aten and the heretic king, Akhenaten. He must have secretly feared that Tutankhamun would one day follow in his brother's footsteps. While Tutankhamun was young he could be manipulated, but as he grew older, Ay would find it more and more difficult to influence events.

Thebes, the city of Amun, once more regained its old grandeur. Akhetaten had been officially abandoned and all the official papyrus records were moved from the archives, while the cuneiform clay tablets, which were too bulky, were carefully buried under the floors, copies having first been made on papyrus. These we know as "The Amarna Tablets" or "The Amarna Letters", and from them we have learned a fantastic amount about the foreign relations of Amenophis III, Akhenaten, Smenkhkare and a little of the first few years of Tutankhamun. The houses of the rich and the merchants were also abandoned, but were stripped of all their valuables before being bricked up. Later, when the police and other security officials had left, the city was inhabited by squatters, who broke into the residences, although the majority of activity was concentrated near the old faience and glass works close to the palace. The rest of the city became a ghost town. With the departure of the guards of the necropolis and the police, many of the tombs in the nearby cliffs were broken into and plundered by tomb robbers. To avoid plunder, a number of burials were removed to Thebes, including those of Queen Tiye, Nefertiti, Smenkhkare, Akhenaten and other members of the royal family who had died at Akhetaten. Thus, at short notice, tombs had to be hewn in The Valley of the Kings to accomodate them. The work would have been the responsibility of Ay as Vizier of the South. These tombs were small and held more than one mummy. Tutankhamun would have officiated at the ceremonies, and would have placed whatever funerary equipment he deemed necessary in the tombs. It appears that these reburials were less rich than their occupants had prepared for themselves, although this would have been inevitable in the circumstances.

During the reign of Tutankhamun, Ay becomes all powerful and although he subsequently only ruled himself as Pharaoh for four years, his period of actual rule lasted for more than thirteen years. Under Tutankhamun, Ay had himself appointed Vizier and Regent, and one Egyptologist has pointed out that Ay also had himself appointed Crown Prince designate, and therefore had the right to succeed to the throne, should Tutankhamun die without heirs. Ay also had members of his family raised to high positions. He appointed Nakht-Min, who is thought to be his son, to the positions of Fan Bearer and General. Many of Akhenaten's entourage disappear from the scene with his death, Ay replacing them with men under his influence, possibly their sons. Important men in Akhenaten's Court such as the Cup Bearer, Parennefer, the Great Chamberlain, Tutu, and the Vizier, Nakht, are not heard of again. This was probably done without malice, although, in the case of one, a certain May, the Fan Bearer, there may have been some attempt to disgrace him. This is suggested by the defacement of his figure in his tomb, but this may have happened at a later date, we just do not know.

Ay, in the name of Tutankhamun, also made efforts to maintain the security of Egypt's border, and appointed General Horemheb, who was responsible for the military security of outlying areas, to the position of King's Deputy. Horemheb was probably a close friend of Ay and a very able man. Together they must have taken steps to re-establish law and order, although by Horemheb's later actions he appears to have been more ruthless than Ay. He was married to Mutnodjme, the sister of Queen Nefertiti and the daughter of Ay. Thus, their friendship was sealed by a marriage alliance.

The situation on Egypt's boundaries, which Tutankhamun found on his succession, was chronic. Under Akhenaten, the State had paid little attention to Egypt's vassal states and her alliances with friendly kings. There was unrest and friction among the lands surrounding Egypt, with many of the allies attacking each other. There was unrest in Palestine and the Hittites were causing havoc, attacking all and sundry and replacing Egyptian domination with their own. Many monarchs chose to ignore Akhenaten and in some cases preferred to communicate with his mother, Queen Tiye, and those who chose to communicate with him usually appealed for help to repel attacks on their territory. To these Akhenaten turned a deaf ear.

During the reign of Tutankhamun, the policing and military activity was left in the hands of Horemheb. At the beginning of the reign, with the aid of a small expeditionary force, Horemheb managed to collect the taxes from Palestine and the Lebanon. It is unlikely that any major wars were waged during Tutankhamun's reign, and the scenes showing him smiting the foes of Egypt, as depicted on the painted chest and other objects found in his tomb, are probably only symbolical. However, order was gradually restored, although Egypt's domination and territories were probably reduced. Horemheb's main task was to strengthen the borders of Egypt itself. A relief on the wall of the tomb of Horemheb, shows Tutankhamun and his Queen, Ankhesenamun, at their State Verandah or Window of Appearances, receiving tribute from nine ambassadors from Libya and Asia. All the ambassadors are paying homage to Tutankhamun, which is being received on behalf of the King by Horemheb, as King's Deputy. He is shown decked with numerous gold collars and holding the fan and insignia of his office. Other reliefs show tribute of captives and slaves.

The internal religious and political situation is outlined by Tutankhamun on the Restoration Stela, which he erected at Karnak in the 4th year of his reign. In describing the condition of the temples on his accession, (i.e. the temples of gods other than the Aten) he says they had fallen into ruin, the shrines abandoned and the buildings overgrown with vegetation and weeds, like a wilderness. He says it was "like as though they had never been". On the stela he acknowledges the

125

faults of his predecessors, which he implies, were due as much to their policies as to their sexual weaknesses. (Homosexuality was not acceptable to the gods, with the exception of Seth, the god of violence and evil. At death, the deceased was normally expected to declare, before the God of Death, that amongst other things he had not indulged in such perversions.) He says that due to their policies the land had fallen into confusion, the gods having forsaken it. Armies met with no success in their campaigns to widen the frontiers of Egypt, and if prayers were offered to a god or goddess they were not answered. The morale of the people was low. Having outlined the state of Egypt on his accession, Tutankhamun then goes on to outline the steps that he had taken, and was taking, to restore the temples and land of Egypt to its former glory. He was re-opening the temples and re-furbishing the sanctuaries. The temples' coffers were being refilled and their property restored. Slaves were again allocated to them so that their daily services could be maintained. Images were being made in gold and precious stones, and new statues to the gods erected. Temple dancers and singers were allocated to the temples and their keep paid for by the King. Akhenaten seems to have done a thorough job in the running down of the temples, for Tutankhamun says on the stela, that he found it difficult to find priests. It is possible that a member of the royal family was appointed to the position of Second Prophet of Amun, as had been the case under Amenophis III and was to be when Ay was Pharaoh.

Thus while Horemheb protected Egypt's boundaries and Ay managed the major affairs of State, Tutankhamun was fully engaged in all the ceremonial duties entailed in the dedication and consecration of numerous images, and temples. Much of the young King's life must have been spent attending religious and official ceremonies. This was according to Ay's grand plan of restoring confidence in the monarchy. The King would have travelled throughout the land, carrying out these tasks, which would also have suited Ay, for while he was thus employed he was unlikely to take the affairs of State into his own hands. When Tutankhamun was not performing these duties, he indulged in his favourite sport, hunting. The young King seems to have enjoyed this, as we can see from the numerous objects buried with him which show him accompanied by his favourite hound, hunting lion, ostriches, etc. He must have been an accomplished bowman for buried with him were several beautiful bows, including a "bow of honour". Other hunting equipment was also buried with him, including a number of boomerangs. His hunting activities must also have been encouraged by Ay, who seemed anxious to keep him occupied with anything except the affairs of State.

The accession of Tutankhamun to the throne also marked the beginning of the end of the Amarna art style, which had been encouraged by his brother, Akhenaten. Art gradually returned to the old conservative styles, though for the greater part of Tutankhamun's reign, still retained something of the earlier Amarna flavour. The art style that developed is typical of his reign and completely disappears during the reign of Ay and Horemheb, returning to the rigid formality of earlier periods. The greatest works of the Egyptian artists of Tutankhamun's era were buried with him in his tomb in The Valley of the Kings, and are today the finest objects of Egyptian art that we possess.

As Tutankhamun grew older, probably due to his religious duties as restorer of the god Amun, he took more and more interest in religion and politics. His early upbringing at Akhetaten had firmly impressed upon his mind the doctrine of the Aten. As an ardent follower, he must have compared the theology of the Aten with that of Amun and the other gods. His adherence to Aten worship is clearly illustrated by the many objects showing the Aten in its developed form, found in his tomb.

This growing fascination must have alarmed Ay, who feared that the new King would show similar tendencies to his brother, Akhenaten. Although the possibility of this seemed remote while the King was young, as he became older and took more interest in State affairs, making his will known, Ay could see that it was a real danger. All his efforts seemed to have been in vain. It must be remembered, that throughout this period the real power seems to have been in the hands of Ay, supported by Horemheb. As Tutankhamun took increasing responsibility for government, Ay could see all his efforts of the past nine years, to restore Egypt to order, were in jeopardy. Thus, when Tutankhamun was eighteen or nineteen, he was in effect actual ruler of Egypt, and Ay reverted to his real position of adviser. Looking back over all these years, we can see that Ay was one of the major threads of stability that spanned the reigns of Akhenaten, Smenkhkare and Tutankhamun. We now see this man faced with a dilemma. His love of Egypt had to be weighed against his love for his nephew, Tutankhamun, and his grandaughter, Ankhesenamun. What was he to do ? The real power was no longer in his hands but in Tutankhamun's. What really happened we don't know. What we do know is that Tutankhamun, at the young age of eighteen or nineteen suddenly died. Whether his death was natural, or whether he met with an accident while hunting, (there was that small scab by his ear, that Dr. Derry had noticed during his examination of the mummy), or whether Ay's love of Egypt overcame his personal feelings and Tutankhamun was poisoned, we shall never know. (The process of mummification would have removed all evidence of poison, so it is not surprising that Dr. Derry felt unable to determine the cause of death.) But it seems that providence again intervened and saved Egypt.

Tutankhamun was buried with much pomp and ceremony and accorded probably the richest burial ever given to an Egyptian King. If Ay did remove Tutankhamun from the scene, it was not through malice, and he made every effort to ensure the young King's welfare in the Nether World. He also seems to have used the burial of Tutankhamun as a clearing up operation of the Amarna Kings. Burial furniture probably left over from the burial of Smenkhkare or usurped from his tomb was included, together with various other objects belonging to members of the royal family. Numerous funerary gifts were included, and Ay took the unusual step of having himself portrayed on the walls of the tomb, like a pious son performing the rites before his father. Ankhesenamun appears to have been heartbroken, and we can remember the little wreath of flowers, which Carter found, that she probably placed on the coffins as a last farewell, before the sarcophagus was closed.

The tomb in which Tutankhamun was buried was probably not originally intended for him, but for Ay, who usurped the tomb originally meant for Tutankhamun in the western branch of The Valley of the Kings. Thus, it was too small to allow some of the burial furniture into the tomb and the lintel and door jambs had to be cut back to allow in the larger objects. It was still too small for the State chariots, which as we have seen, had to be cut into sections.

The activity on the death of Tutankhamun must have been feverish, for although many of the funerary objects had already been prepared, he could not have been expected to die so young, and many of the funerary objects had to be especially made, during the period of mummification. The seventy day interval, the duration of his mummification and funeral preparations, must also have been a period of intense political activity. Tutankhamun had left no surviving heirs. Ankhesenamun had had two stillborn children, who were mummified and placed in small golden coffins in Tutankhamun's tomb. They were both female, and as they had been born dead, bore his name.

The struggle for supremacy must have been intense. There were two possible claimants to the throne, Ay and Horemheb. Although Ay had been declared "Crown Prince designate", he could not have obtained the throne instantly without a military coup, the only peaceful way was by marrying his grandaughter, Tutankhamun's widow, Ankhesenamun. We can imagine Ankhesenamun's plight, and we have firm evidence of her attempt to extricate herself from the situation. She was present at Akhetaten when both Akhenaten and Smenkhkare had died rather mysteriously, and now her own husband, Tutankhamun was dead too. She would have seen the rise to power of her grandfather during the reign of Akhenaten, and his manipulation of State policies during the reign of her husband and may have suspected that Ay's present position was no accident of fate.

The Hittites had been gaining power over the years, influencing some of Egypt's former vassal states. The death of Tutankhamun coincided with an Egyptian defeat in Northern Syria by the Hittites, who, defending their treaty obligations, invaded Egyptian territory between the Lebanon and Anti-Lebanon. Perhaps Ankhesenamun saw a chance to obtain peace in the outlying lands and also solve her own problem of the succession of the Egyptian throne, at the same time. From clay tablets found in the Hittite capital near Boghaz Keui, in Anatolia, we learn that Ankhesenamun wrote to the Hittite King, Suppiluliumas, informing him of the situation and requesting him to send her one of his sons, whom she would marry and make Pharaoh of

Egypt. Ankhesenamun pleads with him, pointing out the situation which surrounds her and saying that she refused to marry just any claimant and that she required a man of royal blood, (son of a King) even if he was a foreigner. The King seemed amazed at this unprecedented request and sent his chamberlain to Egypt to investigate the situation. All this must have been done in great haste. The chamberlain returned, apparently satisfied that the offer was genuine, and Suppiluliumas sent his son, Prince Zennanza to Egypt and Ankhesenamun, at speed. He never arrived. Ay must have uncovered the plan and the Prince was murdered on his journey. Against the superior statesmanship of Ay, Ankhesenamun was no match, and by the time of Tutankhamun's burial we see that she has submitted to her grandfather, marrying him, thus enabling him to be proclaimed Pharaoh. Had Anhesenamun succeeded, the whole course of Egyptian history would have been different.

Ay did not rule for long, only for a period of four years. With his death the common denominator of four reigns disappears from the Egyptian scene. What are we to think of him? Was he ambitious or was he a patriot? Was he a Brutus or a Caesar? The events themselves are known, but it is you, the reader, who must decide. Horemheb succeeded Ay and ruled for twenty seven years, during which time he completely restored orthodoxy to Egyptian politics, religion and art. He strove to strike out all memory of the Amarna Kings and their god, the Aten, and usurped monuments of Ay and Tutankhamun, replacing their names with his own, claiming to be the direct descendant of Amenophis III. He marks the end of the 18th Dynasty and the beginning of the 19th, during which the well known kings with the name of Ramesses ruled, but none will be remembered like Tutankhamun.

Thus the final act in the bizarre drama of the Amarna Kings had been performed. With the burial of Tutankhamun, Egypt must have been confident that he and his brothers, Akhenaten and Smenkhkare, were safe in the Nether World and would be forgotten. For over three thousand years this remained so, until that fateful day in November 1922, Tutankhamun was resurrected in all his glory and thus a minor king of the 18th Dynasty became The Golden Monarch, the symbol of Egyptology itself.

CHAPTER TWELVE

★

CURSE

It is strange but true that men love fiction rather than fact. For even with the fantastic splendours and wonder of the burial of the King, the public had to have something more. They found it in a curse — no curse left by ancient priests, but a curse of the imagination. A strange sequence of deaths of some of the men connected with the excavation, was seized upon by journalists and made headline news. The public, who had devoured with relish the steady flow of news of the excavation, accepted with equal relish the sensational news of the strange mystery of "The Curse of the Pharaoh", as one newspaper put it.

The first victim of the curse, as the newspapers would have it, was the sponsor of the expedition himself, Lord Carnarvon, in April 1923, only a short time after the opening of the tomb. Carnarvon actually died from pneumonia, contracted as a result of fever from an infected insect bite. But to the sensation loving public, he was obviously the first victim of the Pharaoh's curse. Hadn't everyone always known that the dead should not be disturbed ? Especially when they were Egyptian Kings. Memories and imaginations went wild. Inscriptions were recalled, imaginary of course, which threatened those who violated the tomb. Another more practical theory, so the promoters thought, was that

Carnarvon had been infected by an object, left in the tomb for that very purpose, by the guardians.

No sooner than the first victim had been claimed by the curse, than another was taken. This time it was Georges Bénédite, the head of the Department of Egyptian Antiquities at the Louvre. Death was due to a stroke. The third victim died not long after. A. C. Mace was the Assistant Keeper of the Department of Egyptian Antiquities at the Metropolitan Museum of Art, New York, and had been a member of the team, as well as co-author with Carter of "The Tomb of Tutankhamen", published in 1923.

By now, the curse was firmly established and there was no going back. The papers had a field-day. In all twenty-one victims were claimed, among them the son of Lord Westbury, a former secretary to Carter. He was found dead in his bed, through no apparent cause. Perhaps the most bizarre claim for the curse is the death of Lord Westbury himself, who, at the age of seventy eight jumped from the seventh floor of his London flat.

The list of those who did not die, perhaps more than anything else, has helped to lay the legend of the curse, and shown it as it really is, a figment of the imagination, helped by sensational journalism. Carter himself died in 1939 at the age of sixty six. Dr. Derry, who performed the anatomical examination of Tutankhamun's mummy lived to be over eighty, as did Sir Alan Gardiner. Rex Engelbach, the Chief Inspector of Antiquities, later Director of the Cairo Museum, and the photographer Harry Burton, both lived to old age.

In the so called scientific and civilized society that we claim to have today, the presence of unexplained phenomena is uncomfortable. Thus the curse can be dismissed, and we can relax with the thought that it was all myth — or can we ? For there remain two happenings which have yet to be explained, to which the adherents of the curse theory stick doggedly. The first, is that at the time of Lord Carnarvon's death at 1-55 a.m. on the morning of April 5th, 1923, all the lights in his hotel suddenly went out. Not much you will say, a technical failure. Enquiries the following day, however, showed that the lights had failed all over Cairo at the same time. When asked for an explanation, the English engineer in charge of the electricity supply could offer no technical reason.

Also, at the precise time Lord Carnarvon died, his dog in England, suddenly howled terribly and died.

"There are more things in Heaven and Earth, Horatio, Than are dreamt of in your philosophy."

There is an interesting postcript to the story of the curse. The widespread public interest in the imaginary supernatural events, prompted the growing film industry to produce a film inspired by the curse. Made in 1932, it was directed by Karl Freund and starred Boris Karloff as a rather over active mummy. Other films followed, including The Mummy's Hand in 1940, with the sequels The Mummy's Tomb, The Mummy's Ghost and The Mummy's Curse following between 1942 and 1944. The Mummy was remade in 1959 by Hammer films, starring Christopher Lee. Since then there have been other productions including The Curse of the Mummy's Tomb in 1964 and The Mummy's Shroud in 1966.

The myth of the curse, the horror films, all will be forgotten, but the names of Carter and Carnarvon will be remembered for all time irrevocably linked in an eternal tryst with that of Tutankhamun's. As the funerary inscriptions prophesied "To speak the name of the dead, is to restore them to life." Like Tutankhamun, both Howard Carter and Lord Carnarvon are now dead, but their names will be repeated time and time again, and will gain immortality with The Golden Monarch who had died more than three thousand years before.